THE ETHICS OF IVF

ETHICS

OUR
CHOICES

Series editor

Canon Stephen Platten

The series introduces specific subjects of concern and controversy within Christian ethics to a wide variety of readers. Each subject is approached at a serious level, but technical language is avoided. The books should appeal to a wide readership and will be useful in introductory seminary programmes, in programmes for congregational development, and also to individuals seeking information and guidance within their Christian life.

Canon Stephen Platten is the Archbishop of Canterbury's Secretary for Ecumenical Affairs and Co-Secretary of the Anglican–Roman Catholic International Commission. Previously he was a Residentiary Canon at the Anglican Cathedral in Portsmouth and taught ethics for five years at Lincoln theological college; he was also Chief Examiner in Ethics for the General Ministerial Examination of the Church of England. He has published in a number of learned journals including *Theology* and the *Anglican Theological Review*. He was Chairman of the Society for the Study of Christian Ethics at its inception, and has been responsible for forging the very close links which exist between that Society and the Society for Christian Ethics in North America.

The Ethics of
IVF

ANTHONY DYSON

MOWBRAY

Mowbray
A Cassell imprint
Villiers House
41/47 Strand
London
WC2N 5JE

387 Park Avenue South
New York
NY 10016–8810

First published 1995

British Library Cataloguing-in-Publication Data
A catalogue record for this book is available from the
British Library.

ISBN 0–264–67283–6

Phototypeset by Intype, London
Printed and bound in Great Britain by
Biddles Ltd, Guildford and King's Lynn

CONTENTS

Lilian Dyson
in memoriam

Editor's foreword

'The Brangwens shrank from applying their religion to their own immediate actions. They wanted the sense of the eternal and the immortal, not a list of rules for everyday conduct' (D. H. Lawrence, *The Rainbow*). In these two sentences are encapsulated so many of the questions which continue to dominate Christian thought on moral issues. Must Christianity necessarily require of people specific moral responses? Is there a distinctive Christian ethic? How can wider reflections on doctrine be effectively integrated within Christian moral thought? Issues like these and a number of others are addressed in this series of books as we focus one by one on a number of topical ethical questions.

A variety of different stimuli converge upon individuals and communities to press home the questions with continuing force at the present time. Technological advancement and medical research both mean that the empirical data with which we must deal in our moral lives change swiftly and often. The increasing diversity of most Western cultures, where many religions, and none, jostle alongside each other, calls out of the moral agent discernment of what his or her religious convictions demand in such a complex world. Changing gender roles and women's issues raise another set of moral challenges. Dramatic changes in political realities, both internationally and within nations, contribute yet further patterns of what we might call moral vectors. All of these factors mean that ethical issues are being debated with more liveliness than ever. The multiplication of introductory books on Christian moral theory is a function of this accelerating interest.

Recent developments throughout Europe and beyond make the appearance of this particular title in our series most timely. Assisted fertility, sometimes for women beyond the normal age for childbearing, combined with further advances in the associated medical techniques of in-vitro fertilization has provoked widespread controversy. Professor Dyson concentrates specifically upon

vii

the effects of such new scientific capabilities upon our ethical decision making. In doing so, however, he argues for a process of moral reflection that can be applied more widely and indeed which has implications for the moral life as a whole. His critical reflections on the natural law tradition and on the use of the Bible in moral decision making are particularly apposite here.

In an area that requires careful analysis of complex scientific techniques, Professor Dyson charts a course with clarity and without sacrificing either accuracy or detail. He also includes much human reflection from those who have been involved in the process of in-vitro fertilization. He quotes from donors, mothers, doctors and those involved in framing the law. Throughout there is an emphasis on the human and the personal in an area which all too easily can become the reserve of scientists and technicians alone. Professor Dyson, in developing an ethics rooted in respect for persons and responsibility, does not allow individual and social morality to be treated in isolation. Human beings are by nature social and therefore these two aspects of ethics are seen to be part of one integrated whole. In exploring this particular topic we are offered a model for Christian reflection upon ethical dilemmas within the context of an increasingly scientifically dominated society.

Stephen Platten

ACKNOWLEDGEMENTS

I owe a debt of gratitude to a number of people who have helped me to bring this book to completion.

Canon Stephen Platten invited me to contribute to the series of which he is editor.

Dr Brian Liebermann, Consultant Gynaecologist, Regional IVF Unit, St Mary's Hospital, Manchester, has kindly scrutinized the text for medical and scientific errors. Any remaining errors are of course my own responsibility.

Ms Rhoda Hiscox devoted much time and effort in assisting me to prepare the list of references.

My thinking about bioethical matters has been greatly helped by my three colleagues in the Centre for Social Ethics and Policy, Manchester University, namely Margaret Brazier, John Harris and Mary Lobjoit.

Anthony Dyson
Department of Religions and Theology
Centre for Social Ethics and Policy,
Victoria University of Manchester

Definitions

Two terms are introduced at this initial stage, namely 'new reproductive technologies', and 'in-vitro' fertilization (which will be
explained more fully in Chapter 3).

New reproductive technologies

The term 'new reproductive technologies', abbreviated to NRTs,
has become widely used in recent times. A general definition of
the NRTs is 'technologies designed to intervene in the process
of human reproduction'.[1] Another definition refers to 'all forms of
biomedical intervention and "help" a woman may encounter when
she considers having – or not having – a child'.[2] Another definition
speaks of the 'application of biotechnology to problems of fertility
and practices of childbearing'.[3]

Stanworth helpfully divides the NRTs into *four* groups:

- those concerned with fertility control; with preventing conception, frustrating implantation of an embryo, or terminating
  pregnancy;
- those concerned with the management of labour and childbirth;
- those concerned with the management of the ante-natal period;
- those concerned with the promotion of pregnancy through techniques for overcoming or bypassing infertility.[4]

IVF plainly belongs to the last group.

A by no means complete listing of NRTs gives some impression
of the range involved:

- AIH (artificial insemination with the partner's sperm);
- DI (artificial insemination with a donor's sperm. The initials DI
  are preferred to what in the past has been known as AID, to
  avoid confusion with AIDS);

- surrogacy (one woman bearing a child for another woman, where generally the first woman is artificially inseminated with sperm from the partner of the second woman; a variation occurs when an embryo is placed in the uterus of the surrogate);
- amniocentesis and chorionic villus sampling (two prenatal tests; and another test, coelocentesis, at present only in process of development, used to diagnose certain foetal abnormalities);
- embryo replacement (inserting an embryo into a woman's uterus with a view to implantation);
- embryo freezing and thawing;
- ultrasonography (high frequency sound waves used to show visual outlines of internal bodily structures);
- GIFT (gamete intrafallopian transfer where collected eggs and sperm are injected into a woman's Fallopian tubes);
- sex pre-selection (choice of the sex of the embryo before fertilization);
- laparoscopy (visual examination of a woman's ovaries after incisions through the abdominal wall);
- modern methods of abortion;[4]
- pre-implantation diagnoses;
- PZD, partial zone dissection (an aperture made in the egg to allow passage of the sperm).

There is no need to enter into detail about these here. Those which are relevant to IVF will be explained in subsequent chapters.

In-vitro fertilization

The term *in-vitro fertilization*, shortened to IVF, is employed in *four* overlapping ways.

First, IVF refers to *the joining of female egg and male sperm outside the woman's living body.* Hence it is also known as 'external fertilization'. The female eggs (or ova) are placed in a culture medium in a glass or plastic flat shallow Petri dish or other appropriate laboratory container, *not* usually in a test-tube as the popular term 'test-tube baby' describes it. The male sperm is then introduced into the dish and the process of fertilization takes place over the next twenty-four hours or so.

Second, following *fertilization*, some of the embryos are *transferred* to the woman's uterus (or womb), where it is hoped that implantation will take place, followed by a natural pregnancy. These two processes of 'fertilization' and 'transfer' are sometimes called 'IVF and embryo transfer'. Sometimes however, the term IVF *alone* covers *both* fertilization and transfer.

Further, to complicate matters, sometimes a different distinction is drawn, namely between 'embryo replacement' (ER) which is used when the embryo is returned to the woman who supplied the egg, and 'embryo transfer' when the newly fertilized embryo is 'transferred' to a recipient other than the woman who supplied the egg.

Third, sometimes the term IVF is used much less precisely to refer to the *entire process*, beginning with the preparation of the woman for the release of eggs and ending with the delivery of the baby.

Fourth, the term IVF is employed to indicate that the entire sequence is taking place *in and with laboratory apparatus and under laboratory conditions*.

These different usages may appear somewhat daunting. But they are not as difficult as they may seem; the context will usually make the meaning clear.

Introduction

The birth of Louise Brown

Shortly before midnight, on 25 July 1978, Louise Brown was born in Oldham General Hospital, near Manchester. Louise was the world's first baby born after IVF. To use the popular terminology, Louise was the first 'test-tube' baby. This achievement resulted to no small extent from the intense, inventive and complementary collaboration between the Oldham gynaecologist Patrick Steptoe and the Cambridge physiologist Robert Edwards.

Louise's parents, Lesley and John Brown, had for some years tried, but failed, to have children, though John Brown was the father of a child by a previous marriage.

The 12 August 1978 number of *The Lancet* carried, under the names of Steptoe and Edwards, and with the title 'Birth after the reimplantation of a human embryo', a matter-of-fact letter to the editor referring to Louise Brown, but not mentioning her by name. The letter reported that one of their patients, a 30-year-old married woman, was safely delivered, by Caesarean section, of her first child, a normal, healthy infant girl weighing 2,700g. The patient, Lesley Brown, had been referred to Steptoe in 1976 with a history of nine years' infertility with tubal blockages and other conditions.

Amniocentesis (a sample of the fluid which surrounds the foetus is withdrawn and analysed) at 16 weeks of pregnancy had revealed no chromosome abnormalities.

From the Warnock Committee to the 1990 Act

Since 1978, the use of IVF has become widespread, taking up a place alongside the already longer-established procedures of artificial insemination by husband and by donor. Over the last 15 or so years, IVF has retained the interest and curiosity of the media and of the general public.

In many countries IVF has attracted the attention of legislators. In Britain the Committee of Enquiry into Human Fertilisation and Embryology, commonly known as the Warnock Committee after its chairperson Mary (now Baroness) Warnock, was established (some would say, and some did say, that this was none too soon) in July 1982 and officially submitted its recommendations (commonly known as the Warnock Report) to the Lord Chancellor and to five government ministers in 1984. The Report was debated in the House of Commons in November 1984.

After consultation by government, and delays, the Human Fertilisation and Embryology Bill completed its winding and sometimes stormy way through Parliament in 1990.

The Act has three basic purposes, namely:

- first, to provide a statutory framework for the control and supervision of research involving human embryos;
- second, to provide for the licensing of certain types of assisted conception practice, namely those which involve the creation of a human embryo outside the body, or partly inside and partly outside, and any treatment service which involves the use of donated gametes (namely, egg and sperm) or donated embryos;
- third, to effect changes to the Abortion Act of 1967.

The period between the end of the Warnock Committee's work and the legislation for, and the setting-up of, the Human Fertilisation and Embryology Authority (HFEA) was catered for by a voluntary initiative of the Medical Research Council (MRC) and the Royal College of Obstetricians and Gynaecologists (RCOG). This involved the bringing into being in 1985 of the Voluntary Licensing Authority (VLA). In 1989 it changed its name to the Interim Licensing Authority. It laid down 16 guidelines, some of them fairly detailed. The content and procedure of these guidelines broadly followed the Warnock recommendations for 'the establishment of a new statutory licensing authority'. The composition of the membership was also very much along the lines suggested by Warnock and later used in the constitution of HFEA.

We would therefore envisage a significant representation of scientific and medical interests among the membership... It would also need to have members experienced in the organization and provision of services. However, this is not exclusively, or even primarily, a medical or scientific body. It is concerned essentially with broader matters and with the protection of the public interest. If the public is to have confidence that this is an independent body, which is not to be unduly influenced by sectional interests, its membership must be wide-ranging and in particular the lay interests should be well represented... [T]he chairman must be a lay person.[1]

Who are, in fact, members of HFEA whom the Secretary of State for Health appoints? At least half of the membership have to be people *other than* those who: have been or are a registered medical practitioner; have been or are concerned with keeping or using gametes (namely eggs and sperm) outside the body; or have been or are directly concerned with commissioning or funding any research which involves keeping or using gametes outside the body. The medico-scientific group includes a sometime Chief Nursing Officer, experts in genetics, obstetrics and gynaecology, psychiatry, reproductive endocrinology, medical education, mammalian research, and experimental embryology. The other group includes a TV Director of Programmes, a senior lecturer in education, a Law Commissioner, a bishop, a training consultant, a rabbi, an official of the Bank of England, an actress, an expert in family studies, and a Director of Social Services. In the case of the lay members, it is clear that some were chosen both on account of their profession *and* on account of their specialist or personal interest in a field relating to the concerns of the new Authority.

To forward the three purposes set out above, the Human Fertilisation and Embryology Act, having established HFEA, gave it authority to issue three types of licence: a treatment licence, a research licence and a storage licence. IVF is related, in different ways, to each of these licences.

Ethics in the public realm

The debate on in-vitro fertilization from the Warnock Report to the present day has been carried on in the glare of considerable public attention. Why has the topic become so prominent? There are probably many reasons and they are difficult to disentangle. Nevertheless, it is worthwhile making an effort to arrive at least at a provisional answer to this question.

Lord Brabazon's critical speech, about artificial insemination by donor, in the House of Lords in 1943, the Archbishop of Canterbury's separate and negative statement attached to the Report of a Commission appointed by the Archbishop and published in 1948, the debate in the House of Lords in 1949 initiated by the Lords Reading and Brabazon, the 1949 discourse by Pope Pius XII to the International Congress of Catholic Doctors in which he rejected DI, the 1958 Lambeth Conference rejection of DI, the 1960 Feversham Report (of a parliamentary committee) which was comprehensive, of high quality, and which did not recommend legislation — all of these excited more or less temporary, but not sustained, public debate. Which factors led to a different and vociferous response to IVF in the 1980s?

There had been the impact, in the 1960s, of a 'reforming' Home Secretary in matters such as abortion, homosexuality, prostitution and obscenity, which certainly grasped the attention of the media and, thence, of the general public.

Arising out of that experience, and especially the events leading up to the 1967 Abortion Act, was an awareness on the part of those who were opposed to this kind of legislation of how ill-prepared and badly organized they had been, compared with the supporters of those and other measures. During the 1970s, pro-life supporters became much better informed and much more effectively organized to take sides in, and to lead, orchestrated campaigns in the public realm.

The Thalidomide scandal, in which a drug which had previously been used as a sedative was found, if taken during the first three months of pregnancy, to cause foetal abnormalities involving limb malformation, led, with other related experiences, to an enhanced public awareness that the medical profession and, perhaps more to the point, the pharmaceutical industry, sometimes had feet of clay and should be kept under close surveillance.

In the period under discussion, more and more attention was being paid to the notion of 'human rights', not only in general terms but also in relation to smaller and particular groups of vulnerable persons. A pertinent example in the present context was the protest by many women at the control, exercised by doctors and others, of the birthing process which was felt as humiliating in several important respects and as depriving many women of significant elements of autonomous maternal experience.

In the 1960s and subsequently, extraordinary developments in technology, not least in medical technology, pointed to previously unimagined possibilities in respect of human reproduction. But these developments were happening so quickly that time was not available for people to formulate the moral and social sense of what was involved. Furthermore, in these developments, the lines between therapeutic and experimental medicine were frequently becoming blurred.

The five tendencies noted above, to which others could be added, offer some evidence that the movement towards the 'privatization' of morals has not entirely gone the way that some hoped and suspected that it would. The 1957 Wolfenden Report on Homosexual Offences and Prostitution wanted to draw a sharp distinction between public regulation and private morals. Against this, there has emerged from the new reproductive technologies and related practices a widespread, diverse and open debate, which has discussed both private and public ethical issues.

In-vitro fertilization and feminism

A notable feature of the IVF debate in the 1980s and 1990s has been the vigorous and very well-informed participation of many feminist writers. If we compare Simone de Beauvoir's *The Second Sex* (English edn, 1953) and Shulamith Firestone's *The Dialectic of Sex* (New York, 1970) with many subsequent writers, a marked difference can be discerned. Firestone argued that radicals should concentrate their full energies on demands for control of scientific discoveries by and for the people. 'For, like atomic energy, fertility control, artificial reproduction, cybernation, in themselves, are liberating — *unless* they are improperly used.' 'Artificial reproduction is not inherently dehumanizing.' 'We should look for the freeing of women from the tyranny of their reproductive biology by every means available.'[2]

Now I am not aware of any feminist thinker since Firestone who has defended her argument without equivocation. On the other hand, not all feminists who reject her thesis do so equally, though all, including Firestone, would agree that the NRTs, *in our kind of society*, represent in differing degrees a serious threat to woman's self-consciousness — and to her body as well.

This threat can be experienced and described on two levels, though the distinction between them is only for convenience's sake. At the first level, the threatening character of the NRTs can be a cause of damage to the individual woman. But that is not the end of the ethical argument. At the second level, a *systemic* threat is encountered. The woman, whatever may or may not be the outcome for her as an individual, is caught up in, and willy-nilly contributes to, patterns of injustice which affect entire sectors of the world society. In contrast to the highly individualistic arguments employed in much of the literature on the NRTs, the feminist writers have developed a significant body of social ethics instead — a social ethics which must also be reckoned as political to its very core. This perspective, which is present in much of the feminist writing on IVF, will be further explored in Chapters 5 and 10. It is astonishing that most of the contemporary literature on IVF virtually or wholly ignores the feminist arguments.

Why choose to discuss IVF?

Why choose, among the many so-called new reproductive technologies, IVF? This question is easily answered. IVF probably *most* deserves, among the many procedures, the title of 'new reproductive technology'. It is also the most ambitious and the most complex procedure. Of the many procedures, it has probably attracted the most debate. It has also, certainly, the most striking and wide-ranging implications, including embryo research and genetic engineering. It is also a classic instance in the wider debate about the pros and cons of technology.

But why *another* book on IVF? I justify this modest study on a number of grounds.

There appears to be a place for more ethical writing which seeks to mediate between, on the one hand, medical and scientific experts and, on the other hand, a questioning lay audience, including those Christians who are not afraid to treat a number of important questions about IVF as still *open* questions. I shall argue that IVF is, ethically speaking, exceptionally complex and that this is not altogether recognized. I suspect moreover that, by and large, the scientific and medical communities which deal with the NRTs are, with some notable exceptions, not particularly at home in the processes of disciplined moral reasoning, and that many of the rest of us are more or less ignorant about, and uncritical of, science and medicine. This is not a criticism of individuals; but it is a comment about, and a criticism of, what C. P. Snow called 'the two cultures'. These can be experienced in terms of two distinct mentalities or sensibilities which impede the work of ethical dialogue.

I observe in much of the abundant ethical literature a further split, namely between theory and experience. This state of affairs has major ethical repercussions. I refer here, in particular, to the frequent absence of an unembarrassed appeal to human experience, especially emotional experience, as a central source of which moral reasoning ought to take serious and sustained account. How is this absence to be explained? It seems as if theoretical and abstract reasoning belong to the public realm and are fully approved, whilst the different tiers of human, especially emotional, experience are not regarded as ethically respectable, and are thus relegated to the private realm. To give human experience the importance which, in this area, it deserves, I include autobiographical and biographical material woven into the more technical and statistical material.

I shall register in this book a measure of dismay about *some* of the biblical, theological and ethical treatments of IVF which have appeared from Christian sources. It seems that the lessons, coming from over one hundred years of development of the critical method employed on the study of the Bible and tradition, have not been widely heeded. Moreover, some Christians judge that, with biblical and/or theological principles, we can arrive at definitive ethical conclusions without assistance from secular sources of knowledge and judgement. But I am clear in my own mind that neither Christian biblical study, nor Christian theology, nor for that matter Christian ethics, can *by themselves* settle the urgent and difficult questions thrown up by the NRTs, and not least IVF. We need to listen to many different voices.

I attach the greatest significance to the theological principles which will undergird the ethical discussion in the several chapters which follow. But I hold the view that the theological perspective does not emerge from one source. Instead, it comes into being out of an *interplay* of several different bodies of material which include Bible, contemporary scientific knowledge, human experience past and present, political practice, tradition, and the pull of the future. Faithful to this way of proceeding, but limited by space to only a token treatment, I build on the concept of *responsibility*. This concept reflects, illuminates and enhances some of the biblical material. But the concept of 'responsibility' is also a central value of contemporary individual and corporate life, which is formalized in social and political philosophy. Furthermore, in medical and scientific practice, the concept of responsibility is recognized as particularly pertinent.

I have one more preliminary consideration to put before the reader. It is healthy and wise, from the outset, to harbour, not cynicism, but certainly *suspicion* about the rhetoric which is often found in both popular and sophisticated apologetic on behalf of IVF and the other procedures. The appeal to novelty made about the NRTs is not necessarily as innocent as it may seem. According to McNeil, those who want to present the NRTs in this light draw upon 'the myths of progress which so preponderate in Western science generally'. To proclaim the newness of technology expresses the conviction that it is inevitably going to 'transform our lives dramatically and definitively'.[3] Stanworth makes a similar point about the way in which 'reproductive technologies validate the image of science as a realm of boundless progress, bringing triumph over natural obstacles for the satisfaction of human needs'.[4] So McNeil listens with a certain wry suspicion to phrases such as the 'reproductive revolution' and the 'age of the test-tube baby'. On the contrary, she writes 'my own sense of the continuities in the history of medical and social interventions into reproduction make me cautious about such judgements'.

Concerning the chapters which follow

IVF emerged, first of all, as a response to female infertility. Although it is nowadays also used in other contexts, the overcoming of female infertility remains a primary task for IVF. Chapter 1 gives a compressed account of the types and causes of female and male infertility. Towards the end of the chapter, some more detailed comments are made about the condition known as 'tubal occlusions' or 'blockage of the Fallopian tubes', to which IVF primarily responds. In this book, I want to avoid becoming captive to dualisms (body/mind, physical/psychological, reason/emotion). To serve that cause, I interpolate into the text fragments of autobiography concerning infertility.

In Chapter 2, entitled 'Historical moments', I set out to provide some indication of some of the discoveries down the centuries which have, directly or indirectly, been relevant to an understanding of the challenge of infertility. I then go on to narrate a brief history of artificial insemination — a manipulation which, in significant respects, paved the way for IVF. Some readers may be put off by the technical terms employed in this chapter, though they are explained. If this should be the case, they are advised to proceed directly to Chapter 3 and only then turn to Chapter 2.

Many ethical treatments of the NRTs deal only briefly with the physiological, genetic and other processes involved. This makes it very difficult to gain a sense as to what is really involved in the procedure. In chapter 3, I give a reasonably full account of the IVF process. At the end of the chapter, I list some of the ethical objections to the IVF process which will be considered in the ensuing chapters.

One of the objections to IVF concerns the physical risks to the mother and to the embryo-foetus-child. Another objection relates to the low success rates of IVF. These topics are addressed together in Chapter 4. Neither are entirely straightforward matters with which to deal, though they are potentially important from an ethical standpoint.

I have already, in the Introduction, chosen to give special prominence to the ethical attitudes of feminist writers to the NRTs and, particularly, to IVF. I develop this theme in Chapter 5, condensing a substantial body of literature to a few central points.

With Chapter 6, I begin to look at the resources and methods in Christian theology which are in use to investigate the ethical pros and cons of IVF. In this chapter I deal with the concept of natural law. As I shall explain, it is a difficult theme to handle, despite its long-standing centrality to Roman Catholic moral theology. The conclusion of this chapter may come as a surprise to the reader.

Chapter 7 raises questions about the use of the Bible as an ethical norm against which the practice of IVF might be evaluated. Even a liberal treatment of the application of the Bible, such as that of Flynn, cannot resolve all the problems. Simmons provides the basic foundations upon which a more satisfactory pattern of biblical interpretation can be built.

The core of the book is found in Chapter 8. Here I expound an ethical approach to IVF based on the concept of *responsibility*. I then put the concept to use in constructing a way of dealing with the question of the embryo's ethical status — a topic which certainly seems crucial for an ethical study of IVF.

In Chapter 9, I use the concept of *responsibility* to enquire about the different moral agents in IVF, namely the mother and her spouse, the child, the donor and others.

Avoiding a sharp distinction between individual and social ethics, I would claim that the individual-oriented ethic has been dominant in the NRTs. But some writers, including feminist ethicists, have drawn our attention to the problems engendered by the NRTs, not least by IVF, which belong to the wider society. Then Chapter 10, which explores this dimension, links with Chapter 11. This considers the arguments for and against embryo research, which turns out to be a sub-question of the major questions about our ethical attitude to technology.

In the Conclusion, I return to the core theme of responsibility and indicate that IVF is not a marginal issue for Christian ethics, but is part and parcel of the Christian pattern of commitment and responsibility.

1

Infertility

IVF began, and to a great extent remains, a response to female infertility. But now it is also a routine procedure for male infertility. In this chapter, I will give some indication of the nature, scope and consequences of human infertility.[1]

The critics of IVF are bound, of course, to draw attention to the fact of infertility. But it seems that, often, they fail to convey the scale and complexity of the condition, and the mixture of despair and courage shown by those whom it most cruelly affects. Thus no apology need be offered, if the scale of infertility is to be conveyed, for the citing of statistics, even if these are sometimes little more than partly informed guesses.

Moreover, it is important to do some justice to both features of infertility, namely the physical and the psychological. It is frequently the case that far more attention is given to the physical than to the psychological factors. In fact, the physical and the emotional dimensions are very closely intertwined. In order to convey some sense of this intertwining, instead of presenting two blocks of material in sequence, I shall break up the physical data with short passages of autobiographical material. This seems a more imaginative and fruitful way of grasping some of the complex meanings which are covered by the term 'infertility'.

Infertility

Problems with fertility can be described in terms of four stages in the reproductive process. The first stage is concerned with the unavailability of adequate eggs or sperm. The second stage is concerned with failure to conceive. The third stage is concerned with failure to implant. The fourth stage is concerned with repeated failure of early pregnancy.

How is infertility to be defined? Austin defines it: 'in a couple (not attributable simply to a policy of childlessness) the inability of the man to impregnate or of the woman to conceive, owing to causes that may turn out to be correctable'.[2] This leaves the intractable or hopeless cases to be labelled 'sterile'. A widely known definition is that of the World Health Organization. This states that a couple may be considered infertile if, after one year of unprotected coitus of average frequency, no pregnancy has resulted. Some think, however, that the period of one year is too short a time in which to make an adequate diagnosis. Also, some women become pregnant after having been apparently infertile for quite a long time. Another source defines infertility as involuntary reduction in reproductive ability, but that does not distinguish between infertility and subfertility. Subfertility means that at one time fertilization is impossible but later may become possible. A useful distinction is made between primary infertility and secondary infertility. The former of these means that a couple have never produced a child. The latter means that they have become infertile after having had at least one child.

Infertility is put into perspective if it is remembered that most couples are fertile. Around 90 per cent of couples within one year, and 96 per cent within two years, are successful in establishing a pregnancy. But around 45 per cent of all pregnancies are lost before the woman is aware that she is pregnant and at least 15 per cent of pregnancies miscarry. This depends on the age of the woman.

A commonly quoted figure for infertility is that of up to 15 per cent of couples world-wide. The percentage of infertile persons in Western countries is variously estimated as between 5 per cent and 10 per cent. Another source claims infertility as affecting between 5 per cent and 9 per cent of couples of child-bearing age but does not specify whether these percentages are intended as regional or world-wide. The total number of infertile persons, as reported by yet another source, is expressed as one in six couples world-wide or as between 35 million and 105 million. The broad span of estimation again reflects lack of knowledge. It is not clear whether there is a correlation between the fact of a growing medical interest in infertility and the assumption that infertility is on the increase.

How do these overall figures break down between females and males? Some statistics claim that female infertility accounts for between 50 per cent and 70 per cent of all infertility. Male infertility is held to account for 20 per cent to 30 per cent of all infertility.

Male infertility

Male infertility attracted medical attention and research much later than female infertility, namely in the 1940s and the 1950s.

Of the 20 to 30 per cent infertility in men, between 50 to 70 per cent has no known cause. In male infertility of which some causes have been identified, the range of causation is wide, including, for example: several infections (e.g. gonococcus, the causative agent of gonorrhoea, which, if untreated, may spread throughout the reproductive system, causing sterility); swelling of and damage to the testes resulting from mumps; men immunized to their own sperm; environmental factors, including exposure to, e.g., lead, cadmium, mercury and pesticides; injuries; hormonal problems; undescended testes; hypospadias, i.e. a slit along part of the length of the penis through which, at ejaculation, semen escapes; problems with intercourse, e.g. incapacity to develop an erection; vasectomy; too much alcohol; chemicals in cancer treatment; disorders of the sex chromosomes, e.g. Klinefelter's syndrome:

> We knew of one obstacle to pregnancy: Al's vasectomy . . . Al had a sperm count that was in the low normal range . . . [The endocrinologist] is hopeful that husband insemination will work and we are ready to give it a try. I am working hard to maintain some hope in the face of great despair.
>
> (p. 47)[3]

And paraplegia:

> I am an infertile man. I don't make babies . . . My sperm, what there are of them, are immature, malformed, immotile . . . I have known of my infertility for twenty years . . . I vividly remember the indignity and pain of those appointments with the doctor . . . If I cannot give my wife the baby she wants, I do not have anything worthy of giving to anyone I love . . . My wife and I have come to a resolution of our infertility as a couple. We are the adoptive parents of a fine girl who thrives and finds our love . . . I accept my infertility, but I will never, fully, be reconciled to it.
>
> (pp. 38–42)[3]

But whatever the ignorance about causation, it can be confidently asserted that in most cases the symptoms of male infertility are too few sperm (oligospermia), or no sperm (azoospermia), or poor quality sperm.

> I was hoping it wasn't his fault. I was hoping it was my fault because he couldn't handle it like I can.[4]

Male infertility may be tested for in a variety of ways and using a variety of equipment. But the first and vital test is that of sperm analysis in order to establish the sperm count (how many sperm there are in each ejaculate), the motility (how active the sperm are), and the morphology (what the sperm look like). None of these measures predict fertilizing potential. Sperm count is crucial. Several hundred million sperm are probably required for there to be a good chance that one sperm will fertilize an egg. Without a rounded head, a lashing tail, and the capacity to swim well, sperm will be unlikely to arrive at an egg and penetrate it. Second, some hours after intercourse, cervical mucus is taken for analysis to establish motility and how many sperm have reached the cervix. Third, sperm is placed in a dish with hamster eggs from which the tough shell has been removed; it is supposed that the sperm which can penetrate these eggs are capable of penetrating human eggs. This procedure is less used than heretofore.

> A strong desire to become a father got me through my male infertility work-up. Beforehand, I had no idea how awkward and embarrassing a 'medical' procedure could be.[5]

Female infertility

> Most people ask, especially after you've been married for a few years. Society tends to expect a woman to have a family. I found it hard to cope with, and other women I know find it hard to cope with.[6]

The woman's reproductive life lasts from around twelve years of age to the menopause at around 45 years of age, though the prospect of a straightforward conception can diminish after, say, 35 years.

> [The doctor] said that my uterus had been scarred by the Caesarean birth and that an infection had set in. I never had had a chance at another conception. Five years of operations,

tests, inseminations, temperature charts, and drugs had been a complete waste of time and money.

(p. 148)[7]

Infertility among women is more common than infertility among men. Its diagnosis is more demanding and usually requires internal examination. Treatments do not achieve high rates of success.

Five and a half years later, after on-and-off infertility testing, we decided to give it one last attempt, and devote one full year to concentrated testing. By the end of that year, I was emotionally spent ... and still not pregnant myself ... The decision to remain childfree ushered in the worst period of my life ... I was grieving for my loss, but no one could understand ... [Later] many positive changes accompanied being childfree.

(pp. 210–12)[7]

World statistics of symptoms of female infertility, given in percentages, have been estimated at: tubal damage (41 per cent); ovarian failure (38 per cent); endometriosis, i.e. adhesions and scarring from the uterus lining (6 per cent); ovarian, uterine and cervical abnormalities (5 per cent); no known cause (some say 5 to 10 per cent, others say 25 per cent, and others 35 per cent).

The infertility work-up is a gruelling, difficult process and we are right in the middle of it. The 'problem' lies with me and not my husband. I am gradually learning how to cope with my feelings of inadequacy ... My husband ... will be with me when I have a hysterosalpingogram [see pp. 16, 38] next month.

(pp. 49–50)[7]

A number of procedures exist for testing for female infertility.

I do have a real scar ... a lasting token of my laparotomy [i.e. a surgical incision into the abdominal wall] last June. I lost a tube in that operation. My surgeon told me that the bands of scar tissue, or adhesions, resembled a 'Manhattan traffic jam'. I can hardly blame her for sacrificing the tube. Or can I? ... Since then, I have sacrificed my privacy and dignity on the examining table countless times because of infertility ... So far, it has all proved, as they say, 'fruitless'.

(p. 159)[7]

Testing the levels of hormones may give indications whether ovulation is taking place. Laparoscopy, which illuminates and magnifies, can be used to examine uterus, tubes and ovaries. A special dye, injected into the uterus and the tubes, shows up the shape of the uterus and whether the tubes are blocked (hysterosalpingogram). Ultrasound indicates position of tubes, uterus and ovaries.

> After two years without a pregnancy, we sought medical treatment ... There was some indication that I might be experiencing ... [problems with] secretion after ovulation, which interferes with implantation and pregnancy ... I completed this cycle [of treatment], failed to conceive ... [After another cycle, I telephoned] for the pregnancy test results and it was positive! ... I enjoyed a wonderful pregnancy with minimal problems.
>
> (pp. 15–18)[7]

Causes of female infertility include: failure of the ovaries to release an egg, mainly owing to hormonal or chemical problems; adhesions and scarring in parts of the pelvic cavity (endometriosis):

> What I did not understand at the time of diagnosis was that endometriosis meant more than painful periods. In many cases, and mine is one, it means infertility as well ... Had the surgeries and the Danocrine led to a pregnancy, I would surely look back and say it was all worth it. But they did not. I am thirty and childless, trying to hold on to hope, as it grows dim.
>
> (p. 14)[7]

cysts of the ovaries; excessive milk hormone (prolactin); tubal damage; problems of the uterus; problems of immunology; failure of implantation; ectopic pregnancy; primary amenorrhoea (menstrual cycles failing to start at puberty); secondary amenorrhoea (lack of menstrual cycles provoked by undernutrition or starvation (cf. anorexia nervosa), or by prolonged strenuous exercise):

> In some ways it was easier when I was pregnant for the first time. Then I was simply the recipient of a miracle. Hard earned, the result of several surgeries and long, difficult recoveries, but a miracle nonetheless. And after my son was born I returned to my infertility ... Eleven months later, the quiet questions erupted: an ectopic pregnancy, that cruel hoax on those of us who've had our tubes 'repaired'.
>
> (p. 74)[7]

or miscarriage:

> After a year of inconclusive testing, I had two, brief pregnancies that ended in miscarriage ... The infection was treated, and for another year we continued with tests, treatments, and attempts to get pregnant. Then ... another spring, I had my fourth miscarriage ... My husband and I are [now] in the midst of adoption procedures.
>
> (pp. 151–53)[7]

> By the time my tenth cycle had elapsed, we realized that we simply didn't have the emotional stamina to continue any longer.
>
> (p. 157)[7]

There are also psychological causes of female infertility.

Fallopian tubes

In the statistics on female infertility noted earlier in this chapter, the most common problem was tubal damage. In Africa, tubal damage accounts for 85 per cent of all female infertility. It is therefore appropriate to give some details about it.

It is in the ovaries that the eggs mature and from the ovaries that the eggs are released to pass down the tubes.

The two Fallopian tubes (or oviducts) extend from the ovaries to the uterus (womb). Inside they are lined with thousands of small, delicate hairs which push the egg and the sperm — the sperm of course going in the opposite direction to the egg — from the cervix and up the tube.

The most common cause of tubal damage is PID (pelvic inflammatory disease). Micro-organisms enter the pelvic region inflaming the tubes, and also damaging the ovaries and the opening of the oviducts with their delicate fimbria (fringe of finger-like projections) by scarring and blockage.

PID is connected with a variety of factors: in a half to three-quarters of cases with sexually transmitted disease; insertion of IUD contraceptive; abortion; childbirth; surgery; circumcision; appendicitis; ectopic pregnancy; use of a tube into the uterus to withdraw fluid; etc.

Often the Fallopian tubes are totally closed (occluded), preventing access even to the microscopic sperm. Under some conditions, the eggs cannot leave the ovaries nor be surgically extracted.

Yes, but what is infertility?

The 1987 Vatican Instruction *On Respect for Human Life* contains a section on 'The suffering caused by infertility in marriage'. Sections of this significant passage read thus:

> The suffering of spouses who cannot have children or who are afraid of bringing a handicapped child into the world is a suffering that everyone must understand and properly evaluate. On the part of the spouses, the desire for a child is natural: it expresses the vocation to fatherhood and motherhood inscribed in conjugal love. This desire can be even stronger if the couple is affected by sterility which appears uncurable.

> Nevertheless, whatever its cause or prognosis, sterility is certainly a difficult trial.

> Sterile couples must not forget that 'even when procreation is not possible, conjugal life does not for this reason lose its value. Physical sterility in fact can be for spouses the occasion for other important services to the life of the human person, for example, adoption, various forms of educational work and assistance to other families and to poor or handicapped children.

> Many researchers are engaged in the fight against sterility. While fully safeguarding the dignity of human procreation,

some have achieved results which previously seemed unattainable. Scientists are therefore to be encouraged to continue their research with the aim of preventing the causes of sterility and of being able to remedy them so that sterile couples will be able to procreate in full respect for their own personal dignity and that of the child to be born.[8]

The main burden of these extracts from the text is straightforward. Infertility (or sterility) is a suffering, a difficult trial, a sad situation. Plainly, infertility is recognized as a physical condition which merits treatment and research. Where nothing can be done, sufferers may share in the Lord's cross, the source of spiritual fruitfulness and may embark upon alternative personal vocations and ministries.

But there are limits and horizons to be respected. Although 'the desire for a child is natural', 'marriage does not confer upon the spouses the right to have a child, but only the right to perform those natural acts which are per se ordered to procreation'.[8] The last part of the sentence insists that the context and action of producing a child are confined to the inseparable connection between the two meanings of the conjugal act (intercourse), namely the unitive meaning (mutual love-union) and the procreative meaning (procreative potential) in marriage. (Thus provision of sperm by masturbation for procreation is morally illicit.) Coming into being in this way, and in no other, willed by God, the child is 'not an object to which one has a right nor can he be considered as an object of ownership [but rather is] a gift, "the supreme gift" '.[8]

It follows that the method of IVF is unethical and goes against the will of God. Sterile spouses cannot justify a desire to use IVF by appealing to the right to bear a child. Taking the Instruction as a starting-point, I shall now rehearse some objections and questions.

Granted that the aim of medicine is to restore people to a healthy state, in what sense are infertile people unhealthy? Some answer this by saying that in all respects except one, infertile people are biologically functional and healthy. This is not a sound argument. That people are in all other respects healthy does not detract from the fact that in one respect they are unhealthy. Some people say that infertility *is* a disease. In this connection, it seems odd that some people link the notion of a 'need' to have a child with the judgement that infertility is a disease, but link the notion of a 'desire' or 'want' to have a child with the judgement that infertility is not a disease. It is not clear that anything particularly useful is being said in linking a subjective state of mind with whether a condition is to be judged a disease or not a disease.

It seems more sensible to recognize that a disease is a 'cultural construction' which does not have a stable meaning. More productive is the recognition that infertility is plainly a 'malfunction' of which there can, as noted earlier in this chapter, be a legion of causes. But some who accept that infertility is a disease, by dint of its involving a physical malfunction, point to the peculiarity of that disease. Thus, unless one is consciously seeking to have a child, one can essentially remain unaffected by the disease of infertility all of one's life. Yes, but people may equally be preoccupied with their infertility most of their lives.

It is certainly true that IVF does not cure infertility, though it can resolve certain consequences and symptoms of infertility. In the main, IVF circumvents a malfunction. It is perhaps society's exaggerated view of real medicine providing real medical cures which causes some people to play down the circumvention of a malfunction. As in the case of 'real' medicine, there is the need to establish whether the practice of IVF is sufficiently high up on a list of priorities to justify time and expenditure, and also whether, as a circumvention of a malfunction, it is or is not ethical in other features too.

2

Historical moments

I mentioned in the Introduction that it is thoroughly misleading
to imagine that IVF somehow has no history. 'To earliest man the
propagation of the race and its survival was a source of real
anxiety; a woman who failed to conceive and carry a pregnancy
to term was a source of concern and she regarded her plight as a
disgrace.'[1] Even as technology, today's IVF is not strictly novel; it
is only possible because of earlier research, discovery, reflection
and technology. In this chapter I shall present, in a highly
impressionistic and compressed way, some relevant 'moments'
from both the more distant and the more recent past. The reader
is not encouraged to pore over details nor to become preoccupied
with technicalities. But I do want to convey, at this early stage, a
sense of the human ingenuity, persistence and achievement in
responding, from different angles, to the challenge of infertility.
Thus, Edwards and Steptoe's contribution was a major and
notable climax of a long, but of course unfinished, history.

Every country has customs and folklore concerning the relief of
infertility. Hindu women, who passed through a hole in a rock or
cloven tree, symbolizing the female birth passage, would (they
hoped) have improved fertility. Ceremonies were employed to keep
at bay demons which caused deformity in the infant.

In Persian writings, Anaitis, the moon goddess, was also the
goddess of birth. She purified the male seed, watched over
the foetus, provided mother's milk and ensured an easy labour. In
Chaldea and Babylon, infertility was ideally suited to beliefs about
astrology and numerology. Thus libido and menstruation were
controlled by the moon.

In Greece, the goddess Eileithyia had as her symbols the
moon which promoted procreation and growth, and the cow
because of its fertility. Fertility could be tested thus: 'If a woman
do not conceive, and wishes to ascertain whether she can conceive,
having wrapped her in blankets, fumigate below with oil of roses

and if it appear that the same passes through her body to the nostrils and mouth, know that of herself she is not unfruitful.'

Chinese and Javanese women were given dried placenta to eat to improve their fertility. (The placenta is the organ by means of which the embryo is attached to the wall of the uterus. As a gland, it secretes, among other things, chorionic gonadotropin which is used in infertility treatment today.)

Rome took over much Greek medicine and did not contribute much of its own. An exception was Soranus who practised in Rome (98–138 CE) as an obstetrician and gynaecologist. He described accurately the female pelvic organs and pioneered the use of the vaginal speculum. (The speculum is an instrument for inserting into and holding open a cavity of the body, in this case the vagina, to examine the interior.) He also identified the time shortly after the menstrual period as the most favourable for conception. After Galen (130–201 CE), who was more influential, but less distinguished, than Soranus, medicine fell into general decay.

In the period 1000–1500 CE, obstetrics was largely in the hands of midwives. The publication (c. 1540) of The Byrth of Mankynde led to improved midwifery.

A popular recipe designed to promote conception was composed of 'syrups of Motherwart and Mugwort, spirit of Clary, root of English Snakeweed, Purslain, Dates, Pistaches, Conserve of Succory, Cinnamon, Saffron, Conserve of Virvine, Pineapple-kernels picked and pilled'. Names of importance in obstetrics in the 1600s were Harvey (de Generatione Animalium, 1651), Eustachius, Fallopius (cf. Fallopian tubes), and de Graaf (cf. Graafian follicle).

Of major importance for the understanding of reproduction was the microscope. Using homemade microscopes, Anton van Leeuwenhoek made the first drawings of spermatozoa. In 1786 Spallanzani showed that spermatozoa were essential to fertilization. He also suggested the freezing of human semen.

Still in the eighteenth century, Wolff showed the development of the egg from its early cell-divisions onwards.

In 1752 Boehmer observed that previous sterility might be related to the later development of an ectopic pregnancy. In the late eighteenth and early nineteenth centuries it was concluded that certain physical conditions were associated with infertility and that the Fallopian tubes could be a cause of sterility. In 1849 a British gynaecologist, Tyler Smith, attempted to catheterize the Fallopian tube. (The catheter is a long flexible tube for inserting into a bodily cavity or passage.) In 1827 van Kolliker demonstrated the origin of spermatozoa in the testicular cells, and that the sperm fertilized the ovum which then underwent segmentation. (Segmentation refers to the repeated division into a solid ball of cells.) Van Kolliker also suggested that hereditary characteristics were carried by the cell nuclei. In the same year, von Baer discovered the mammalian ovum and took Wolff's work further.

Sims, an American, in his 'masterpiece' *Clinical Notes on Uterine Surgery* (1866), separated gynaecology (the study of diseases of women and girls, particularly affecting the female reproductive system) from obstetrics (the branch of medical science concerned with the care of women during pregnancy, childbirth and the period about six weeks after). The *Medical Times and Gazette* criticized him for 'dabbling in the vagina with speculum and syringe ... [which was] incompatible with decency and self-respect'.

In 1839 Schleiden judged cell-formation to be the universal principle of the organism. Schwann concluded that mammalian eggs were essentially cells. It was supposed that eggs were formed by a spontaneous process.

In 1800 Humphry Davy suggested the use of nitrous oxide for anaesthesia. Later ether and chloroform were introduced.

The new knowledge of pathology opened the way to gynaecological surgery. (Pathology is the branch of medicine concerned with the cause, origin and nature of disease.) Gonorrhoea as a cause of sterility in the female was explained by Noeggerath in 1872. In 1903 Davis and Varnier discovered the sterilizing effects of X-rays on human ovaries and testicles.

From the end of the nineteenth century and beyond, there were a number of relevant surgical experiments. For example, in the Estes operation (named after W. L. Estes), ovaries are grafted into the walls of the uterus so that eggs are produced straight into the uterus where they are fertilized by natural intercourse or by AI.

In the same period, techniques were developed for investigating the pelvis and the reproductive organs without a major operation. This would lead to laparoscopy (see 'Definitions' at the beginning of this book), whereby ovary and follicle could be directly visualized.

But the modern era of infertility may be said to have begun only in this century with the studies of Huhner on sperm survival in the cervical mucus, the test for tubal patency (the tubes being free from blockage) described by Rubin in 1920, the development of the modern concepts of menstruation by Allen and Doisy in 1924, and a description by Moench in 1931 of semen characteristics associated with infertility and fertility. These studies, encompassing the area of the cervix, the endometrium (mucous membrane lining the uterus), the ovulatory factor, and the male factor, remain today the backbone of diagnosis and therapy.[2]

Fertilization of mammalian eggs, from rabbits and guinea pigs, was apparently first attempted by the Austrian embryologist S. L. Schenk in 1878. In 1879 Walter Heape showed that it was possible to make an embryo donation from one female to another. Heape used an Angora doe rabbit and a Belgian hare. Gregory Pincus, an American, with E. Enzmann, reported success with fertilizing rabbits' eggs around 1930, though this claim was challenged.[3] Pincus certainly recognized the possibility of maturation using a suitable culture or nutrient, as three decades later Chang recognized the need to copy the process of capacitation in the sperm which, in nature, occurs in the genital tract. (Capacitation is the process by which the surface of the sperm is conditioned so that it can penetrate the egg's hard outer layer.) Pincus may have been the first to try IVF with human eggs. In the late 1940s John Rock in Boston, with Menkin and Hertig, at the end of many years working with hundreds of eggs taken from poor women at Brookline's Free Hospital for Women, reported that he had developed embryos to two- and three-cell stage. In the 1950s, Landrum Shettles in New York circulated photographs of artificial conception, and, with others, was confident that infertility could be treated by IVF. Daniel Petrucci in Bologna, also in the late 1950s, claimed success in fertilizing women's eggs and was ready to transfer an embryo to a woman in 1961. He met, apparently, difficulties with the Roman Catholic Church. M. C. Chang, at the Worcester Foundation in America, undoubtedly produced IVF rabbits in 1959. Robert Edwards worked intensively on egg maturation and culture media in the early to mid 1960s. In 1969 Edwards reported the external fertilization of human eggs, viz.

seven out of 56 eggs. It required nearly ten years of further dedicated work before the first IVF baby was born under Edwards and Steptoe's supervision.

Two undergirding areas of research and discovery must be mentioned: first, the rise of molecular biology in the 1940s and the elucidation of the structure of DNA by Watson and Crick in 1953, showing the basic principles of how a species can reproduce its own kind; and, second, the development of endocrinology (the study of the endocrine glands, which include the ovary, the testis and the placenta, and the substances which they secrete), shedding light upon the reproductive cycle and the human menstrual cycle.

Taymor draws attention to what is still of great significance today, although put forward by Meaker in 1934, namely the recognition of the complex nature of infertility diagnosis and treatment. Meaker wrote about the 'multiplex nature of causation' and 'the division of responsibility between male and female partners'. 'These two principles and their utilisation in practice still continue to provide the greatest impetus to success in diagnosis and therapy.'[2]

Historical moments of artificial insemination

It is sensible to include some historical reference to artificial insemination in this chapter since that procedure and IVF have a good deal in common. Much of the technical knowledge acquired through the practice of artificial insemination was useful in the development of IVF.

There are references in the Jewish Talmud and Mishnah which may have more to do with accidental impregnation of women than with insemination proper. But medieval writing about the birth of Ben Sirach suggests that in that era something was known about the principle and practice of insemination. In the fourteenth century there is mention of impregnation of Arabian mares and of sheep. The fertilization of fish eggs in the fifteenth century was attributed to Don Ponchom and in the eighteenth century to Jacobi. Around 1550, it is reported, Bartholomeus Eustachius, Professor of Medicine in Rome, advised a wife to persuade her husband, after coitus, to push the semen up towards the mouth of the uterus. John Hunter, the celebrated English clinician, is credited by some as one of the first to apply insemination to humans, possibly around the end of the eighteenth century. In 1777, Spallanzani, Professor at Pavia, inseminated toads and, later, dogs. In 1865 Dehaut published a pamphlet on 'artificial fecondation'. A more scientific approach was developed by Girault between 1838 and 1861. Marion Sims in America performed insemination in 1866. Harley was carrying out active experimentation in England around that time. France was the most active country in this regard. The first German publication appeared in 1879.[4]

While the first mention of a donor is apparently in 1900, the first publication about DI appeared in *Medical World* in 1909. This is the much-discussed case of Professor Pancoast's successful insemination of a merchant's wife in Philadelphia after her husband had been found to be infertile. There is however doubt on the part of many about the veracity of this report. For reasons which are not clear, published cases of DI were much more common in the United States than in Europe during the first decade of the century. Also not explained is the public preoccupation with AI in Germany in the 1910s, with France in the 1930s, and in England in the 1940s.[4]

An early British publication going into some detail is the article 'Artificial insemination' by Barton, Walker and Wiesner in the *British Medical Journal* in January 1945. It gives a careful account of the scope and the procedure of insemination. The following features deserve attention as anticipating later debates.

> ... the husband's brother might be regarded as the first choice because of genotypical resemblance; but experience shows that this choice is usually incompatible with secrecy, and that it is conducive to emotional disturbances involving both husband and wife. In fact, the prospective parents should never be aware of the identity of the donor.

> ... the donor is never described to the patient save in most general terms which exclude identification.

> If he [the donor] wishes to limit his donation to certain types of patients his wishes are, of course, considered.

> The principles which govern the choice of donors are designed to reduce obvious biological dangers.

Our choice has favoured men of intellectual attainments whose family history indicated that the members of at least two preceding generations were not only intelligent but also endowed with good capacity for social adjustment.

The donor should have at least two legitimate children; this is of importance not only from obvious genetic considerations but also because his parental drive will have an available object. He must be of mature age (30 to 45), so that his character, viability and other qualities can be properly assessed.[5]

Complementary, yet in tension

Thus IVF and DI have things in common, such as the timing of the procedure in relation to the woman's cycle and the use of donors. Notwithstanding, important differences should be noted. Despite (to some extent successful) efforts to medicalize DI with searching preparatory physical and psychological screening, and very formal, clinical inseminations, there are evidently counter-tendencies. One example is the domestication of AI with the administration of semen intimately (literally!) linked with lovemaking at home.

Yet there is a more radical, even anarchic, phenomenon. While hospital and clinic DI centres often impose conditions such as marriage or stable partnership, a woman is in fact free to seek semen where she wills, whether from a friend or institutional source, and in the circumstances she wills. Likewise DI is open to the desires of homosexual partners, male or female, and of single parents, to 'have' children without reference to the medical profession, often at little or no cost, away from the disciplines of informed consent, and in personally chosen conditions.

We have seen that through many centuries and in many cultures the inability to have a child has been a source of much anguish. Only in the latter part of the twentieth century has medical science, based on distinguished antecedents, made it possible for more than a few people to circumvent infertility.

3

The IVF process
and its ethical problems

The IVF process can be divided into four phases. The first phase is concerned with the production of eggs (or ova). The second phase is concerned with the extraction of eggs. The third phase is concerned with fertilization (or conception), and the fourth phase with the transfer of the embryo to the mother's uterus (or womb).

There are problems of presentation in this chapter. Too much detail will ensure that the reader will probably not see the wood for the trees. Too many technical terms will have the same effect. However, as will become apparent in the ethical sections of this book, enough information about the IVF process is required not only to enable some overall ethical judgements to be made, but also for more particular ethical judgements about the phases and sub-phases of the process. Furthermore, in dealing with the process and its phases, data relevant to the theological theme of *responsibility* must be continually borne in mind. They will be called in evidence later on when judgements about responsibility will be made. So, in this chapter, somewhat more than the minimum of description is included. Conventional medical terms are used, but brief explanations or one-word, non-technical, alternative terms are supplied.

Many of the feminist writers also mention the question of IVF terminology to important effect. Suffice it to say here that a middle course should be steered between language which reduces the IVF process to nothing more than mechanisms and language which sentimentalizes or disembodies the process.

In this chapter, the use of interwoven autobiographical material will again be employed, for the psychological and emotional responses to the process are probably even more in evidence in this chapter than they were in Chapter 1.

Preliminaries

I had all the usual tests done — everything from A to Z. After years of tests and two operations, the end result was absolutely nothing — unexplained infertility. I went to another infertility specialist to get a second opinion and was told, 'Relax, keep trying'. They couldn't find anything. I always thought they were implying that the problem was in my mind, and, although I didn't think so, I would wonder. . . . I kept thinking I had to do something, find more information, see other doctors, or else nothing would happen. It was so frustrating to keep calling or writing people, because it takes so much emotional energy to do that. But I did it anyway because I wanted a baby so badly. Finally, one doctor suggested I try in-vitro.[1]

Women and men often have resort to IVF after a long history of trying to overcome infertility by other means. Before the woman is admitted to the IVF process, the procedures are explained in detail, usually to the partners. It is important to assess the psychological as well as the medical characteristics and histories of the woman and man, to establish whether they have the degree of toughness to cope with the ups and downs, the tensions and the possible disappointments of the process. Medically, hormone analysis and testing of sperm and of cervical mucus (a fluid secreted by the mucous membranes at the neck of the uterus) are carried out. The condition of the woman's reproductive organs is assessed. It may turn out, for example, that the woman's ovaries are not accessible for manipulation. Informed consent is usually required of the spouses.

The production of eggs

A common pattern has been for the woman, early in her menstrual cycle, to take Clomid (clomiphene citrate) which diminishes the effect of oestrogens (hormones that control female sexual development) already present in the woman's body. This leads the pituitary (the master endocrine gland) to release its hormone which stimulates the follicles (sacs in which eggs develop in the ovaries). Next, the woman has taken menotrophin. This is a powerful fertility drug, the dosage of which may have to be increased if the ovaries do not respond. Newer drugs in use now reduce objectionable side-effects.

[After the fertility drugs] I had unbelievable, unbelievable headaches. Like nothing I'd ever had in my life. I could not work. I could barely keep my head up... I could hardly concentrate on my studies with the Pergonal. I could hardly keep up with my school work.[2]

There will probably be a daily blood test and an ultrasound scan. The scan will monitor the development of the egg follicles, as well as checking that the ovaries are not being excessively stimulated by the Pergonal. If it is clear that the hormone levels are rising and that eggs of sufficient size are developing, the woman will be ready for the egg extraction between, say, day 11 and day 14 of her cycle.

At every stage I was terrified that I would fail and not make it to the next step. I was scared and upset.... There was also the feeling that I didn't want to say anything because I would be jinxed.... Then they told me the time looked good to release the eggs from the follicles.... It really drew me in when I saw those eggs on the surface of my ovary in the ultrasound.[3]

If the development of follicles is not satisfactory, the whole process will halt. The woman may begin the first phase afresh.

I'd been there for a week and things were not looking very good. The eggs were not developing the way they wanted them to. That was hard to take. Here the nurse is telling everybody after the ultrasounds to come back tomorrow. Then she sits down quietly in a corner with me and says, 'Well we're sorry to have to scrap this cycle'. It was like someone had died.[4]

If the evidence is such that ovulation is near, an injection of HNC (human chorionic gonadotrophin) will be given to trigger ovulation (release of an egg) to happen 30–40 hours later.

The extraction of eggs

'Egg-extraction' is probably the most straightforward and accurate description for the next stage of the process. The terms 'egg collection', 'egg harvesting', 'egg pickup', and 'egg retrieval' are also used.

The timing of the extraction is all-important. If the woman should happen to ovulate before the egg-extraction can be performed, she is of course not able to proceed to the next phase of the normal programme. The extraction must take place shortly before the already induced ovulation.

> I think it was more of a rude awakening, because it had gone so well in July and I went through the whole program. How the hell did I get canceled? So you go through a lot of what did I do wrong? I didn't do anything.[5]

There are two main methods of egg-extraction, namely laparoscopy and ultrasound-directed recovery.

The first, and established, method (developed to a high level of sophistication by, among others, Patrick Steptoe) is laparoscopy — a surgical procedure. The laparoscope, similar to a slim telescope, is a fibre optic instrument, say 10mm in diameter, which is inserted through an incision made normally just below, or through, the navel. The laparoscope can relay pictures of the inside of the body for direct observation. Two more incisions are made, one for small forceps which will search for and hold the ovaries, and the other for a hollow needle through which the eggs are sucked out (aspiration). 'The art of egg harvesting ... lies in piercing the follicle with the hollow needle while at the same time using a foot-operated vacuum pump to gently suck out the egg.'[6] The procedure requires a general anaesthetic and the distension of the woman's abdomen with a carbon dioxide gas mixture to allow the organs inside to be seen more clearly. The operation takes, on average, about 30 minutes.

The second method, trans-vaginal ultrasound-directed oocyte (egg recovery), also known as 'ultrasound egg pickup', is initiated with the woman's bladder being emptied with a catheter (flexible tube) and refilled with saline solution. A needle for extracting mature eggs is inserted either through the abdominal wall and via the bladder, or through the vagina, thence moving towards the ovaries. An ultrasound picture helps the doctor to identify the right location. The eggs are sucked out. Either heavy sedation or local anaesthetic can be used. The procedure can, in principle, be carried out on an out-patient basis. The extraction can possibly yield around 20 eggs; all of these will be extracted.

> I went into surgery for the removal of the eggs. When I woke up, the doctor told me they had gotten three eggs and they looked pretty good. I felt a tremendous sense of relief at that point. The worst part physically was over — the ultrasounds, the driving back and forth, and then the surgery.[7]

Laparoscopy is reported to be successful in about 80 per cent of cases.[8]

The fertilization of eggs

The eggs which have been extracted are washed; the follicular fluid and the red blood cells are removed. The eggs are put in one of a number of culture mediums, e.g. a simple salt solution with the woman's serum (the fluid which separates from clotted blood or blood plasma) in a glass dish for observation. Defective eggs are not used for fertilization.

The remaining eggs incubate for five to 18 hours at body temperature. About two hours before the time when the sperm is to be joined to the eggs, the sperm is collected from the man by masturbation. It is possible that he will be advised to ejaculate, say, four days before fertilization and not ejaculate again until he provides the semen. In this way, the semen will be fresh for the fertilization. Then the sperm is washed free of semen, tested for count and motility, and incubated, in a parallel culture fluid, for one to two hours. Usually 100,000 motile sperm are added to each egg which are both put in the incubator. During this stage the sperm sheds the coat around its head (capacitation) to enable it to fertilize the egg. Later the eggs are checked for fertilization and, if successful,

> That was horrible, horrible to go through... the doctor came down [and] his whole face shows his emotions and he just looked at me and he goes, 'Not good news'... He said,

'they're no good. They're not going to fertilise. You can go home.' And I just burst into tears in front of everybody, and I'm not like that. I couldn't help myself.[9]

the embryo is placed in a fresh culture medium for another 24 hours. Subsequently the two nuclei fuse. The result is the embryo. After another six hours there is a two-cell embryo; after another twelve hours a four-cell embryo appears and after 14 to 20 hours later an eight-cell embryo. At two-, four-, or eight-cell stage the embryo is ready for transfer.

I burst into tears when the nurse called and told me eggs had divided. I realised I had finally created new life.[10]

The replacement of the embryo

This brief procedure is called embryo replacement. Some 48 hours after the egg-extraction, the fertilized eggs, probably three in number, if still developing correctly, are returned to the woman's uterus. (That no more than three embryos should be returned to the uterus was Guideline 12 of the 1988 Report published by the Voluntary Licensing Authority, the interim body established after the Warnock Report:

Consideration must be given to ensure that whilst a woman has the best chance of achieving a pregnancy the risks of a large multiple pregnancy occurring are minimised. *For this reason ... no more than three ... pre-embryos should be transferred in any one cycle, unless there are exceptional clinical reasons when up to four may be replaced per cycle.*)[11]

An ultra-thin plastic catheter (flexible tube) or a cannula (hollow tube) containing the embryos is inserted through the cervix and the embryos are flushed out into the uterus. No anaesthetic or sedation is usually required. The cervix is not usually dilated. The natural hormone progesterone is sometimes administered; it prepares the inner lining of the womb for implantation. It should be noted that the effect of the catheter passing through the cervix may be that the cervical mucus which has previously 'closed' the uterus will open it, and that the embryos might escape. Sometimes the woman is kept in hospital for 24 hours.

The worst time is definitely the two weeks between when you get out of hospital [after the embryo replacement] and your period. There's nothing that can describe what you go through, the mental torture you put yourself through.[12]

Afterwards

Twelve days later a blood test is done to establish whether the embryos have implanted. In view of the low success rate of IVF, and especially of implantation, most women will have a negative result from their test; some will be aware already of this outcome since their menstrual period has come before the test.

When you get your period... you can't believe it... and when it doesn't work, that's when you curse everybody. You feel depressed. You're not worth anything.[13]

The 'happy ending' is as follows:

I seemed to have had a miscarriage about two months before I conceived my first child, almost a year and a half after we began trying to conceive... It seemed as if I had been trying to get pregnant forever. In retrospect, after having worked for ten years with infertile couples, I now know that I am one of the lucky ones. A year and a half is small potatoes in the cosmic realm of infertility.... I began to enjoy my pregnancy more once I believed it was real. I finally had the baby for whom I longed and who I never believed would be mine.[14]

The 'far-from-happy ending' is tersely narrated.

The doctor called and said, 'I'm sorry, it's not positive'. I got off the phone and I wanted to bawl. I was just shaking. And I had to wait until everyone left the house until I finally [broke down].[15]

Objections to IVF

While the IVF process is still fresh in the mind, I shall list summarily and without comment several principal ethical objections to IVF, some of which will be analysed, at greater or lesser length, in subsequent chapters of this book. I shall not distinguish here between objections which are primarily religious and those which derive primarily from other sources. In any case, that distinction is sometimes almost impossible to make. The first objection is an example of a first-order objection. It derives from the Roman Catholic tradition. All the others are treated as second-order objections. The wording of the objections does not necessarily reflect my own choice; they are intended to represent the kind of standpoint which the objector might adopt. I am aware that, to be fair, the wording of the objections requires qualifications. I have, however, preferred to keep them in an immediately accessible form.

- IVF disrupts the connection between the emotional-union meaning and the procreative meaning of the sexual act and so diminishes the divinely given dignity of the human.
- IVF requires, for the development and continued improvement of the technique, the use and destruction of many embryos.
- IVF often introduces third parties into the process.
- IVF can result in genealogical confusion, especially in the children.
- IVF can lead to deception within the family as the price to pay for the preservation of anonymity.
- IVF sometimes involves embryos not being transferred to the uterus but rather being destroyed.
- IVF frequently leads to the freezing and thawing of gametes and embryos with, it is claimed, untoward consequences.
- IVF involves the commodification, commercialization and exploitation of persons and processes.
- IVF involves women in serious physical and/or psychological risks.
- IVF's low success-rate is incommensurate with the risks to mother and embryo, and with the use of expensive resources.
- IVF involves, it is said, embryos and foetuses in higher than normal risks.
- IVF may cause psychological and emotional disturbance for donors.
- IVF is the current way of producing large numbers of embryos for the purposes of research.

- IVF opens the way for genetic therapy and for eugenic practices, intensifying an already abortionist culture.
- IVF dehumanizes, by medicalizing, the reproductive process, especially for women.
- IVF undermines the values of the 'traditional family'.
- IVF fosters embryo sex-selection, and therefore more abortions of unwanted embryos.
- IVF processes are invasive of women's privacies.
- IVF reinforces a greater resort to, and a greater confidence in, technology.
- IVF fosters the fallacious expectation that perfect 'consumer-designed' children can be brought into being.
- IVF breaks into the continuity (conception, gestation, birth) of woman's reproductive consciousness.
- IVF, if taken to its logical subversive end, will change the balance of power from the traditional, dominant authorities of patriarchy to a new dominating authority, the 'technocrats'.
- IVF lies on the route to ectogenesis (artificial womb) and thus to femicide.

4

Risks and successes

Chapter 3 offered a fuller account of the IVF process than appears in most of the non-technical literature. The word 'process' was deliberately used, in the title of that chapter, to describe the total sequence of IVF. It is also appropriate to regard the human interventions which occur within the IVF process, not as isolated, external, intrusive events, but rather as sub-processes intimately linked in with the patterns which begin with the separate egg and sperm, and end — if all goes well — with the safe birth of a child.

Notwithstanding, the technical interventions of IVF bear major and weighty responsibilities in the overall process because of the vital functions which they perform, namely in the sub-processes at critical points. These relate to ovulation, egg-extraction, external fertilization, and the replacement of the embryo in the uterus.

What outcomes follow these technical inputs which serve as auxiliaries to, and triggers of, the 'natural' developments of pregnancy?

Answers to this question can come under two headings, namely the calculation of *risk* to which the woman and child in the IVF process are exposed, and the degree of *success* which IVF registers in producing live babies.

Risk

Fisher, in his book *IVF: The Critical Issues*, quotes a 1984 statement by a senior figure in the American College of Obstetrics and Gynecology to the effect that IVF 'has become a standard part of medical practice. The risks to the mother, even after repeated attempts at egg-retrieval, are minimal.'[1] This kind of statement hinges on the word 'minimal' and on the criteria which establish it. But, whether referring to 1984 or to today, broadly speaking it is a case of acute understatement.

But there is a second consideration. Fisher, in the same book, observes that 'IVF is still too new for us to judge accurately how "safe" it is or what its long-term effects will be'.[2] This sounds a more prudent judgement than that of the American spokesperson referred to above. But what does one conclude from Fisher's observation? Any new medical procedure in principle carries risk. But there comes a time at which, if safety in the short run appears to be secure, one may legitimately proceed routinely. However, the long-term consequences of IVF arise from carrying out the procedure and waiting for the long term to arrive. What does Fisher want to say — that it is a matter for experimentation in the short and the long runs and so (as Paul Ramsey avers) should not be proceeded with at all?

A third consideration, of a different order, concerns the connection between risk and the woman's willingness to be exposed to that risk. Some women — the argument runs — are so eager to achieve a pregnancy that they will put up with a much higher degree of risk than will the average woman in less charged circumstances.

Some examples of risks to the mother are now listed:

- Pregnancy carries increased risks as the woman comes close to the end of child-bearing age. IVF women are commonly in that category.
- Clomiphene, a drug which has been widely employed for the purpose of ovulation induction, can cause, e.g., severe headaches, blurred vision, nausea, uterine bleeding, weight gain, hair loss, constipation, dizziness, insomnia, hyperthyroidism, rashes, and abdominal distension and pain. Some fertility drugs result in cysts forming on the ovaries which are painful and can cause bleeding. There can be a link with gastrointestinal symptoms and disorders, and further, with haemoconcentration (diminution of intravascular volume), renal failure, and coagulation disorders. Fertility drugs can also be related to abnormalities in the woman's ova.
- Laparoscopy, used for egg-extraction, may cause, e.g., subsequent abdominal pain, infection, and haemorrhage. In rare cases, the bowel is damaged. There are general risks linked with surgery and anaesthesia, including a low risk of death (1 in 30,000).
- Hysterosalpingography, used for radiography of the interior of

the uterus and of the Fallopian tubes, is painful for some women. There is a small risk of infection.

- The use of a catheter to replace embryos in the uterus can carry bacteria which may cause infection, and can cause damage.
- Risk of psychological illness related to IVF is more difficult to identify and appraise. The vulnerability to 'stress, anxiety, disappointment, depression, pain, exhaustion, disruption of work life and social life, strain on marriage and finance' in IVF will almost certainly express itself in one form or another. But similar features may well be experienced by infertile women who are not undergoing IVF and by male partners who may or may not be infertile.

In addition, these maternal risks look high when compared with those in the day-to-day life of non-pregnant women. But compared with the risk attaching to women undergoing a 'natural' pregnancy, the scale of IVF risks is obviously less striking.

Risks and the IVF child

It is claimed that there are heightened risks for the IVF child, as against the 'natural' child. But there appears to be a variety of views. Some of these risks seem to relate to multiple pregnancies and can be included where an IVF multiple pregnancy is involved, but not in the case of an IVF single pregnancy. To time, financial cost, psychological stress and physical problems, in different forms and degrees for the mother, may be added the heightened risks for the IVF child, as against the 'natural' child, which some experts believe that they have detected. But again there is no consensus. Some indications can be given, it being understood that the samples are not large and the findings are only tentative.

- Perinatal mortality (namely still births, and deaths in the first 28 days after birth) in IVF babies has been estimated as four times higher than the general norm. Even when that figure is adjusted to take account of the higher maternal age of some of the women involved, the mortality rate is still, it is alleged, double the general norm.
- Pre-term delivery and low birthweight are more common in

IVF than in natural conception. These are directly related to multiple births.

- Ectopic pregnancies, which kill the foetus, and, probably, spontaneous abortion, occur more commonly in GIFT than in naturally conceived pregnancies.
- Some argue that the incidence of major congenital malformations and chromosomal abnormalities seems to be no higher in IVF than in the general population. But this is, in turn, contested with claims for the higher incidence of physical and mental retardation, and for abnormalities which include, for example, defective cytokinesis (the last stage of cell division), skeletal and growth problems, heart and lung disorders, brain disorders, kidney problems, digestive system disorders, ear nose and throat problems, gland and genital disorders, and risk of siamese twins.

Experimentation and failure rates

We have seen that a first major argument raised against IVF, and chiefly associated with the name of Paul Ramsey, insisted that the procedure was experimental and that there was a quite unacceptable risk in subjecting embryos to this experimentation. In Ramsey's view, this was an overwhelming reason for not pursuing IVF.

But the success with Louise Brown in 1978 led IVF supporters to claim that IVF was now an established therapy and that the argument based on the experimental character of IVF no longer carried weight. This claim to an established status involved two assertions. First, the Ethics Committee of the American Fertility Society expressed the view in 1986 that success rates with human IVF techniques had steadily improved since the first birth in 1978.

This assertion was, however, called into question by another study in the United States which estimated that fewer than half of the 169 centres offering IVF had ever created (sic) a baby.

The second assertion came from the MRC/RCOG to the effect that IVF should be regarded as a therapeutic procedure covered by the normal ethics of the doctor/patient relationship. As Ellis asks, 'Is IVF experimental, or is it a proven medical therapy?' This question is too simple by far.[3]

IVF is presented and used as if it were a 'proven medical therapy', but the statistics of failure belie that. If it is not a proven medical therapy, it seems right to assume that it is experimental. But it seems often to be experimental only in a half-hearted way, though there are some important exceptions to that judgement.

> From a broader perspective, it is hard to imagine using the label of therapy for a procedure with a success rate of less than one in ten per trial. The efficacy of IVF, despite the fact that it has been used to produce thousands of babies, is still very, very poor.[4]

This leads to the conclusion that to merit the titles of normal therapeutic procedure *and* successful experiment, significantly greater resources should be committed to research.

It is, therefore, hardly surprising that, since the beginnings of IVF, the matter of success rates has been a cause of misunderstanding, dismay and, sometimes, alas, deception. Thus, writing in 1990, Barlow et al. observed that 'infertile couples faced with the possibility of using assisted conception can easily be confused by the variety of types of statistic which might be presented to them both by doctors and the lay media'.[5] A classic example of this is the uses of the term 'pregnancy' (as set out by Laborie): (1) biochemical pregnancy, also known as preclinical or menstrual abortion; (2) clinical pregnancy; (3) ectopic pregnancy; (4) ongoing pregnancy ending in spontaneous abortion; (5) completed pregnancy.[6] (There is no need to be more precise, instead simply to note that the term 'pregnancy' covers events from a few days to, say, 20 weeks.)

On the problems of IVF statistics, Jones and Rogers confirm that 'the end results from IVF programmes are difficult for the reading public to ascertain — and, indeed, sometimes difficult for those involved in a programme. Unfortunately, the results are also subject to manipulation.'[7] Barlow et al. want to cut a clear path through all this confusion. They propose an unambiguous and readily comprehensible statement of criteria which can be presented as *so many take-home births per treatment cycle expressed as a percentage*. This seems undoubtedly the formulation which IVF parents and the general public want to know. When does the 'treatment cycle' in this formulation begin? It begins when the woman comes into specific medical infertility care and the first concrete steps are taken which will lead, it is hoped, to successful ovulation.

Another factor which makes for confusion is the different meanings to be attributed to the discrepancies in results between different institutions. For a number of reasons this is not straightforward. It may be that an IVF centre is only in the earliest setting-up stage so that its successes are few. But, depending on the quality of the centre, it may in due course become very successful. Again, it may be that the narrowly selective medical policy of one centre leads to low success-rates so that it compares unfavourably with other centres which have a broader policy. As far as selective medical policy is concerned, the Voluntary Licensing Authority Report for 1991 drew attention to several centres with very low success-rates. But the 'most common finding was that those centres tended to treat more difficult cases, such as older women and couples with male factor infertility'.[8]

Current trends

Using material from the Reports of the Human Fertilisation and Embryology Authority, the following basic statistics are presented:

IVF live birthrates per treatment cycle
1985–90 (all centres)[9]

Year	%
1985	8.6
1986	8.6
1987	10.1
1988	9.1
1989	11.1
1990	12.5

However, there is extreme variation between and within different sizes of centres. Thus the mean percentage of live births per 100 treatment cycles for all sizes of centres, i.e. 12.5 per cent for 1990, includes the low extreme of 0.0 per cent and the high extreme of 22.9 per cent. The corresponding percentages for 1986 were 0.00 per cent and 16.00 per cent.

The more promising figures do not of themselves negate critical judgements on what are, overall, still poor results for an allegedly established procedure. Increased resources for IVF research still seem an urgent need.

5

Feminist critiques of the NRTs and of IVF

This chapter deals with some elements of the feminist critique of the NRTs in general and of IVF in particular. For, without doubt, the feminist criticisms are weighty and demand attention. Surprisingly, very few of the books and articles about IVF make any reference at all to the feminist challenge. As far as my reading goes, feminists are correct in observing that none of the male-centred criticisms of the NRTs, be they conservative or radical, has opposed the technologies because of what they do to women.

The feminist critique is not original to feminism in all respects. But, for the feminists, it is ultimately the ground on which their criticism is based which is decisive. In other words, the feminist critique must reflect the tenets of feminism. This can be tersely expressed as follows: feminism criticizes the NRTs and IVF insofar as these establish or reinforce ideologies, beliefs, attitudes or behaviour which discriminate against women.

This lack of response to the feminist objections to IVF is one reason for giving these a certain pride of place in the contents of this book. But there is another equally important reason for doing so. The feminist critique of the NRTs and IVF is in part a critique of Christian practice and of Christian-ethical theory, not least because the Christian Church has been deeply involved in the medical tradition from the earliest times. It is important to listen to this critique. If it turns out to be soundly based, then we have to reckon with the possibility that in all or some respects the Christian arguments are skewed.

But feminism does not speak with one voice; there is a broad spectrum of conviction. Berer wrote thus in *Spare Rib* as far back as 1985: 'If you ask ten feminists what they think about surrogacy, you'll get eleven opinions. Few women say they are sure of what they think, and many of us have changed our minds three times

43

already.'[1] Similarly, Andolsen, in 1989, in her discussion of the NRTs speaks of '... the growing pluralism within the feminist movement'.[2] Wacjman, however, correctly holds that there are two main types of position which can be constructed for the purposes of discussion. The first type sees 'the development of reproductive technologies as a form of patriarchal exploitation of women's bodies'. 'This technology is intrinsically an instrument of domination.' 'Technology is not neutral. ...' The second type emphasizes, on the other hand, the ambivalent effects that the NRTs have on the life of women. So, it is argued that many of these innovations (the NRTs) offer 'indispensable resources upon which women seek to draw according to their circumstances'. 'These new technologies are seen as having the potential to empower, as well as to disempower, women.'[3]

Following this introduction, some of the primary feminist arguments relating to IVF are now set out.

Feminist arguments

Feminist writers want to show how IVF today stands in continuity with the sexist history of medicine and the sexist medicine in history — including Christian history. Finkelstein remarks that 'women's relationship with scientific medicine has long been unhappy'.[4] She adduces how, for example, before the feudal period, women legally practised as doctors in Spain, Italy and Germany. In thirteenth- and fourteenth-century France, women doctors were also legitimately in practice, although in 1423 a decree passed on the instigation of male doctors excluded all women from that role. Before the eighteenth and nineteenth centuries when male doctors took over virtually the entire healing role, there intervened witch-hunts, persecutions and discriminatory decrees, the rising incidence of illness among women with the arrival of industrialization, the epidemic proportions of puerperal fever among hospital deliveries attended by doctors, and the new degree of dependence of women upon doctors with the arrival of analgesics. Thus, according to Finkelstein, women's contribution to medicine has been progressively devalued and marginalized.

But, there has emerged over the last 20 years an ever-growing corpus of historical studies giving solid evidence for that 'unhappy relationship'. Some of this corpus is detailed, scholarly, exact historical research. Other parts of the corpus are more secondary in character and explicitly polemical, but none the less valuable for that.

The principal conclusions of this corpus are that women's contribution to the practice of medicine has, on the initiative of male society in general, and male medicine in particular, been progressively devalued and marginalized; that the control of women's reproductive medicine has been wrested from women by men; that masculinist philosophical-scientific presentations of women's reproductive biology have distorted fundamentally the image of womankind with the consequence that greater control has been gained over women's social future. Thus the judgement is made that 'the medicalization of female existence, begun with the nineteenth-century establishment of the specialities of gynecology and obstetrics, becomes outrageously solidified in the new technologies of reproduction'.[5] More particularly, the woman who extended herself beyond customary social roles was, in some sense, ill and needing medical treatment. Among such treatments were pelvic surgery, clitoridectomy and removal of ovaries, which would make women more moral, 'tractable, orderly, industrious and cleanly', and otherwise receive relief from their symptoms of social marginality. This history is brilliantly evoked in Mary Daly's *Gyn/Ecology*, which, according to the author, is primarily concerned with the mind/spirit/body pollution inflicted through patriarchal myth and language. I shall give a few samples.

'The self-appointed soul doctors [priests and gurus], mind doctors [psychiatrists, ad-men and academics], and body doctors [physicians and fashion designers] who "specialize" in women are perpetrators of *iatrogenic disease*', '. . . are by professional code causes of disease in women and hostile to female well-being.' 'This book criticizes patriarchal institutions.' The text is divided into three 'Passages' of which the five chapters in the third passage are important for present purposes. 'Indian suttee: the ultimate consummation of marriage'; 'Chinese footbinding: on footnoting the three-inch lotus hooks'; 'African genital mutilation: the unspeakable atrocities'; 'European witchburnings: purifying the body of Christ'; 'American gynecology: gynocide by the holy ghosts of medicine and therapy'. '. . . Gynecology arose in the nineteenth century as a direct response to the first wave of feminism.' 'The spate of gynecological activity in America . . . [was]

characterized by flamboyant, drastic, risky, and instant use of the knife.' 'The castrating doctors saw themselves as reimposing order upon women whose disorder consisted in deviation from the female role of subservience to their husbands and dedication to household duties.'[6]

The first type of feminist criticism identified by Wacjman sees IVF as but the latest in a disastrous historical sequence of medical controls over women. The second type, while not rejecting that reading of history, sees both positive and negative features in IVF.

All the feminist writings lay great emphasis on the physical and psychological risk in the new procedures. They also draw attention to the high failure-rates of IVF. That the 'superdocs' had other motives than helping women to overcome infertility is demonstrated by the very small amount of research undertaken on animals before the IVF procedure was used with humans.

> As a federal ethics board which held hearings on IVF noted in 1979: 'Experts appearing before the Board agreed that there has been insufficient controlled animal research designed to determine the long-range effects of *in vitro* fertilisation and embryo transfer. The lack of primate work is particularly noteworthy in view of the opportunity provided by primate models for assessing subtle neurological, cognitive and developmental effects on such procedures.'[7]

There is a difference of view about the reasons for this relative lack of animal research. In one sense that debate is now past history; in another it is not. For the feminists would expect to find, and claim they do find, a similar pattern emerging with more recent NRTs. Price comments:

> public and published disputes in relation to IVF are not, in essence, about technical risks or about safety or efficacy. They are about perceived and potential social risks and 'slippery slope' arguments ... The IVF procedure raises fundamental ethical questions about the control of human reproduction and the grounds for limiting clinical freedom.[8]

Another feminist conviction asserts that the medical argument is, at base, also a political argument. Writing about the United States, Petchesky claims in relation to abortion that it is 'the fulcrum of a much broader ideological struggle in which the very meanings of the family, the state, motherhood and young women's sexuality are contested'.[9] As Post and Andolsen say, 'the concern is not so much with the technology itself as with its social-political context'.[10] Furthermore, the feminists see in the public debate about the NRTs, evidence of an exceptionally individualistic notion of self-determination in moral decision-making. This is apparent in the case of surrogate motherhood where emphasis on the free consent of the individual woman takes little or no account of the negative influences coming from society at large, which must surely limit that individual freedom. McCormack links this to the debate about ethics, saying that the bias of medical ethics is its 'conservative stance which criticises individual behaviour and individual motives rather than the social order'.[11] Against this McCormack ventures the judgement that 'the problems of reproductive technology are a sub-set of population-policies'.[11] In his influential book *The Gift Relationship*, Titmuss understood that giving was influenced by the relationships set up, social and economic, between the system and the donor which were in turn strongly determined by the values and cultural orientations permeating the donor-system and the society.

Technology is a powerful weapon. To transfer human conception to a technological environment extends the range of male domination over women's bodies and their reproductive power. So one of the areas of debate is whether reproductive technology can be controlled by women rather than men. Warren takes a middle way: 'Women should, therefore, be at least equally represented in the development of these technologies.'[12] Rowland suggests that if these technologies were in the hands of women whose bodies they most immediately affect, we might be able to utilize them to free women and give them new choices. But she admits that 'adding more women to science and technology will not achieve anything'.[13] Hanmer and Allen map out this option in more detail. 'Women need to involve themselves by finding out what is going on. Feminist women in science are needed to inform women continually of scientific and technological development.' 'We must take scientific research and technological developments out of the hands of men.'[14]

Not surprisingly, under the rubric of 'control', some feminists alight on the three reproductive methods (of which two are currently available) where women are not subject to male control.

The first of these is DI, which, unregulated, allows women a measure of control over reproduction and threatens male authority. The second of these methods is surrogacy which, like AID, can put power in women's hands. Could this explain the vehemence of the opposition to *all* surrogacy? The third of these methods is parthenogenesis, namely the development of an organism from an unfertilized egg. The point is that parthenogenesis in mammals would produce only female offspring.

The feminist movement has laid great store by 'women's experience'. Likewise, in much feminist ethics there is emphasis on 'difference', from men's experience and also as a source of, sometimes, distinctive moral insight. So in reproduction women's role is more burdensome, but yields a special knowledge. In this connection, some feminists make much of the notion of 'reproductive consciousness' and argue that for men reproductive experience begins with the alienation of the sperm from the male body. Only after nine months does the male re-enter the reproductive process, not as a continuously genetic father, but now as the social father. For women, however, reproductive consciousness is a continuity from conception, through gestation, to birth. But the NRTs tend to alter and split this consciousness.

All this relates closely to the theme of exploitation of women by the NRTs and, in particular, by IVF. Various forms of exploitation are suggested by feminist writers: that women are exploited for research, and their anxieties about motherhood manipulated; that the dangers for those who serve as experimental subjects are ignored or minimized; that the 'assaultive nature' of IVF requires women to expose their bodies for tests and procedures, and expose the intimate details of their sexual lives and of their motivations for pregnancy. Possible consequences of this exploitation could be: that children will be thought of exclusively as products; that women may be valuable merely as breeders; that reproductive prostitution may emerge as women are forced to sell wombs, ovaries and eggs; that, with the development of artificial wombs, there is the apocalyptic possibility of femicide (systematic killing of women); that, with a greater proportion of males because of sex selection, the prospects of women's access to social and economic power will be entirely eliminated.

Steinberg

The feminist critique of the NRTs and of IVF provides a context in which the specific critical ethical interpretation of IVF can be placed. Steinberg's essay on 'The depersonalisation of women through the administration of *"in vitro fertilisation"* '[15] is an analysis of some of the terms used in IVF. Steinberg decodes the meaning and structure of IVF treatment and language to show how they represent the consciousness and priorities of the medical scientific community about the status of women, their perception of their own legitimate power, and the nature of the IVF project. Steinberg points to two fundamental processes by which the status of women is constructed and reflected in the context of IVF. These are 'erasure' and 'recombination'. 'Erasure' refers to the processes which obscure or remove women from recognition in IVF; 'recombination' refers to the effects of IVF procedures on women, namely the alteration, removal and reconstruction of parts of, or affecting, women's whole bodies. Steinberg holds that both these processes 'operate to depersonalise, that is to fragment, alienate and injure, women'.

1. 'In-vitro fertilization' and 'test-tube baby'

The term 'in-vitro fertilization' names the part but not the whole; it names the one part of the process from which women are physically absent! The term 'test-tube baby' not only misdescribes the Petri dish which is normally used; more importantly, the term 'test-tube baby' ignores the mother's agency and names only the product of the process, namely the baby.

Steinberg draws the conclusion that both of these terms, 'in-vitro fertilization' (with its Latin jargon) and 'test-tube baby' (with its reference to laboratory paraphernalia), implicitly claim that reproductive language belongs primarily, if not exclusively, to the domain of medical science. Leading on from that, the two terms communicate that it is the medical and scientific practitioners who are the agents of IVF, 'the ones who make it happen'. 'Women ... are not only *not* identified as agents of their reproduction, but they are not identified in any capacity.'[15]

2. 'Egg-recovery'

This is a term widely used to name the process in which by laparoscopy or by ultrasound ova are 'taken' from the woman for subsequent fertilization in vitro. This term 'egg-recovery' implies the 'regaining' of something, whereas 'dispossession' might be more precise. Nor do the alternative terms 'egg-recovery' or 'egg pick-up' refer, Steinberg observes, to the woman whose ova are removed.

How does Steinberg summarize her conclusions about language?

> Practitioners use misleading language to name and describe IVF tools and procedures such that 'IVF' appears to be a practice unrelated or, at best, inconsequentially related to women. With 'IVF' treatment, they actively dis-integrate women's bodies and limit women's agency ... Women ... have had no directive or initiatory impact on the development and practice of 'IVF'. Choice for women in this context is, at best, a derivative, consumerist choice. Women can consent to pre-existing options which they have had no substantive role in determining.[15]

What has been said of language can be said of *image* too. 'The image of a disembodied embryo ... still depends, as it has in the past, on the [socially constructed] image of motherhood, not the realities of motherhood.' One such image appears on the front cover of Caroline Berry's *The Rite of Life: Christians and Biomedical Decision Making*. A child's face-head, inside something which looks like a glass wine carafe, but is presumably intended to look like a laboratory container, is linked to no one, not even to the mother. This image recalls Petchesky's observation that:

> the foetus ... could not possibly experience itself as if dangling in space, without a woman's uterus and body and blood stream to support it. In this respect, every fetal image ... is an artificial construct, a *fetish*, representing the standpoint of neither an actual foetus nor a pregnant woman but a male onlooker.[16]

Conclusion

Recalling Wacjman's second type of feminist argument against the NRTs and IVF, Warren believes that, under certain conditions, for example by protecting individual civil rights, the dangers of NRTs being used as ways of achieving eugenic goals can be overcome. Then, 'IVF is probably a justifiable means of attempting to overcome infertility'; 'it is too soon to conclude that this new reproductive technology will not serve women's interests.'[17] Warren argues, however, that the publicity afforded to the NRTs deflects attention from *preventable* causes of infertility. She ventures the opinion that the main feminist objection to the NRTs is that they neglect more effective ways of dealing with the problem.

This chapter has briefly indicated how the feminist writers have approached the ethics of IVF. In the feminist writings, ethics is not seen as a 'spiritual transaction' which takes place between an individual and a divine being nor as a relationship expressed in disembodied language. In the feminist material, context is everything. But that context is composed of many relationships and roles which have to be sorted out with care. For that reason, the social and historical perspectives of IVF are centrally important. The feminists are preoccupied with resisting reductions of the human being, especially the woman, in matters of reproduction. But the feminist task is onerous. For that task is situated, if the arguments are sound, within an exceptionally long and pervasive male-centred tradition of science and medicine.

6

IVF and natural law

The problem

In this chapter, natural law will be examined as the first line of ethical approach to IVF. Natural law is a comprehensive theory which is, arguably, capable of judging IVF unethical root and branch.

This happened to contraception in Pope Paul VI's encyclical *Humanae Vitae* where, ostensibly on the basis of natural law, artificial contraception was found to be unethical without exceptions. Another reason for giving natural law pride of place is that it has been, over many centuries, a very influential tradition in Catholic thought and among quite a number of theologians in other parts of Christendom too. Furthermore, since Pope Pius IX, natural law has been frequently and strenuously appealed to, at least until the Second Vatican Council which challenged natural law in significant respects. The reader may be surprised that an entire chapter is devoted to a rather negative treatment of natural law. But this leads to some very positive assertions at the end.

Natural law theory appears to have many palpable advantages. There is its apparent simplicity. It is widely taken to mean that 'God has visibly set forth God's laws in nature and humans should obey them'. There is also natural law's apparently rational character. Natural law theory does not come from a special revelation from God. All human beings, regardless of their belief or unbelief, can understand natural law. Natural law, therefore, is seemingly ecumenical — in the broadest sense of the term. So, if natural law theory is as convincing as all this suggests, and if it in fact can rule out IVF as unethical at one fell swoop, then there will be no need to explore the ethics of the many secondary issues in IVF.

It must, however, be emphasized at the outset that, despite the apparently rosy picture painted in the previous paragraph, natural law theory has, in the modern period, found fewer and fewer supporters outside the Roman Catholic Church tradition, and more and more critics within that tradition. Some quotations bear witness to this increasing unease about natural law.

D'Arcy writes that 'versions of natural law theory have appeared throughout the history of systematic thought in the West, and they exhibit enormous diversities'.[1] Flynn asserts that 'a perusal of moral literature leads one to conclude that natural law is very difficult to define both in its history and its substance'.[2] Fletcher claims that 'almost all the English natural-law works are, and always have been, of the indeterminate and prospective kind — this and that "will be" or "could be" or "should be" or "needs to be" worked out! They have wrestled helplessly with the dozen different meanings of the term "nature" and the equivocations it introduces into all discourse in which it is used.'[3] Ryan has written that 'on the traditional concept of natural law it is hardly possible to go into the complicated story of its historical development. This history has often been written, and it contains chapters about which there is little agreement among scholars.'[4] Finally and provocatively, natural law has been judged to be a body of doctrine that is 'so vague as to be useless or so biased as to be menacing'. These quotations suggest that not all is in fact as straightforward with natural law as it seems at first sight.

Features of natural law

What are the key features of IVF which come under scrutiny from natural law? The primary feature is undoubtedly concerned with IVF as 'external' fertilization. That is to say, the primary accusation coming from natural law will focus on the fact that in IVF fertilization occurs *in vitro* in a glass dish, rather than *in vivo*, namely in the woman's body. But, though it may not seem so important at first sight, a second feature of IVF which is challenged by natural law is the use of masturbation by the husband or donor to provide the sperm without which the external fertilization cannot go ahead.

Granted that nature is essentially good — because it is God's creation — then the most basic tendencies in the natural order must be tendencies to the good. One such tendency is the inclination in human beings, shared with animals, to procreate. So 'natural' sexual union in animals and humans tends towards the 'end' or 'goal' of procreation.

Thus, for many exponents of natural law theory, what happens in the order of nature outside humankind strongly influences how the norm for humankind is expressed. It is for this reason that some of the critics of natural law have described this aspect of natural law theory as 'physicalist'. In other words, in matters of human sexuality and procreation, human beings are primarily defined in terms of the biological 'nature' which they have in common with the animals. Ryan puts this pointedly as follows: 'Here the natural law seems to come much closer to the idea of animal instinct. Even today when people speak of natural law they may sometimes be found to be supposing that it refers to what is natural in us as against what may be thought of as planned, regulated and artificial.'[5] This quotation is of cardinal importance. Later on it will be necessary to examine more closely the contrast between 'natural' on the one hand and 'planned, regulated and artificial' on the other hand.

The critics of natural law are clear that we cannot 'read off' the rules and principles of living which are appropriate to human beings, especially in the realms of sexuality and procreation, by inspecting what is going on 'out there' in the natural order. Quite the contrary! We have to look at ourselves and at other humans. But the same error lies in wait when we begin to do that. For again, there is the crucial distinction to be made. We do not look at ourselves or at other humans in order to 'read off' objectively binding and universal laws. As Kelly stresses, '[We must reject that mistaken] approach to natural law [which] would maintain that by finding out how we function naturally as human beings (biologically, sexually, genetically, psychologically etc.) we discover how God wants us to live'.[6]

Instead, we reflect upon our own experience, and upon the experience of others, upon what is involved in being human persons. And, arising out of that reflection, we formulate and construct norms which are appropriate to our historical existence. (The term 'historical' in this context does not refer to the past, but to life lived existentially in the finitude of this world.) These historical norms are in no way universal and do not pertain to the eternal law, as the norms of classical natural law theory claim to do. The content of these personal and historical norms will be influenced by a wide range of circumstance and will change as cultures and circumstances change. Included among 'circumstances' will be inventions and discoveries which make the world a significantly different place from what it was heretofore. Then, with our human freedom of action, limited but real, we can ponder whether, in a particular case, we follow or deviate from the precepts which we have formulated and constructed.

It is abundantly clear that natural law conceived along these lines is light years away from the notion of natural law described at the beginning of this chapter where God sets forth God's universal laws in nature and we obey them. Leaving to one side what must surely be called a primitivist account of natural law, we turn to ask how an alternative view may be developed which is fitted to respond to questions posed by IVF.

Reconceiving natural law

Classical natural law theory can be visualized on a vertical scheme on which there are several 'levels'. The first, and 'highest', level is very general indeed and may be regarded as of universal application. At the second level there are rather less abstract applications of, or deductions from, the first-level principles. These second-level principles would almost certainly not be universal in scope because they are shaped by changing cultural norms and other circumstances. It would then be possible to take another step to conceive of, and formulate, third-level principles of natural law which would be yet more concrete and particular, and therefore would admit of even more varieties and exceptions.

Now the important question arises as to the nature of these steps from above to below, from first, to second, and to third levels of principles.

It seems to be the case that the first-level principle in some sense contains the second-level principle, and that the second-level principle in some sense contains the third-level principle. This means that the lower principles are inferred from the higher principles. This seems to have been, and in some quarters still seems to be, the way in which the classical natural law has been worked out. The consequences are that the lower-level principle is 'read off' from the higher-level principle. Disastrously absent from this procedure is any attention to empirical evidence and experience. Moreover, the deductive relationship between, e.g., first- and second-level principles, means that as the first-level principle represents absolutely God's will and purpose, so does the second-level principle without diminishment. But, rejecting these simplistic steps from level to level, O'Connell argues that, on the contrary, 'the attempt to formulate third-level norms [of natural law] is a task involving considerable risk and a significant possibility of error'.[7] An example may be taken from monogamy and polygamy.

Classical natural law theory would presumably assert that monogamy represents, without exception, God's will and purpose, though the fact of some of the Old Testament patriarchs being polygamists led to certain qualifications among some theologians. If, however, we take the view, based on careful empirical enquiry, that monogamy is appropriate to some cultures and polygamy to other cultures, do we then have to say that God rules that each is ethical in respect to its own culture?

But the challenge of IVF to natural law is more complex than the issue of monogamy and polygamy. IVF is such a recent phenomenon that it is not beyond the bounds of possibility that some of the changes resulting from human bio-cultural evolution may transform the relation between humans and nature. Certain acts may therefore attract a different moral evaluation.

So if we approach IVF — in particular, external fertilization and masturbation — with this kind of principle in mind, we should not expect to 'read off' an ethical judgement from the 'given process of nature' in the way this was done as early as 1897 when the Holy Office, with Pope Leo XIII's approval, answered negatively the query whether artificial insemination could be applied to a woman. Instead, completing the quotation cited earlier, we observe that Kelly concludes:

> The [traditional] view I have been describing does not accept this position. It does not believe that 'meaning' is written into 'nature' in this way. It believes that nature is to be read — and the very reading is an interactive and creative process in which the human mind plays an indispensable interpretative and creative role.[8]

This leads to Schillebeeckx's trenchant formulation which radically shifts the entire focus of the argument about IVF. He has proposed a

> personal instead of a biological interpretation, so that the

'nature' to be respected becomes not the reproductive process but 'what is worthy of a human being' — freedom, planning, control of physical nature to serve human nature![9] . . . Man's vocation is actually to frustrate nature as do medicine and technology, if rational needs and purposes require it.[10]

This chapter has shown that traditional natural law theory is too problematic to be allowed the last word about the moral legitimacy of IVF. IVF *may* therefore be interpreted as 'what is worthy of a human being, namely freedom, planning, and control of physical nature to serve human nature'. Whether IVF *ought* to be so interpreted will provide more and more of the subject-matter in the remaining chapters.

7

IVF and the Bible

We turn now to the second traditional resource and criterion in relation to a Christian ethic. If natural law has played its role mainly (though by no means exclusively) in Roman Catholic Christendom, the other influential resource and criterion, namely the Bible, has been found, until recently at least, mainly in Protestantism.

I want to give some indication of the contemporary views held about the authority and interpretation of the biblical writings for Christian ethics, relating them all the time to the question of IVF. Three such approaches deserve mention.

Three ethical approaches to the Bible

First, the American ethicist Stanley Hauerwas, who has little or no sympathy for IVF, nonetheless writes as follows: 'There is nothing in Scripture that says, "You shall not commit *in vitro* fertilization." '[1] It must be added that nowhere in the Bible is the practice of IVF commended.

The reason for this biblical silence is plain. Nothing was known about IVF in biblical times. The practice becomes feasible only in the twentieth century. So, it seems, the biblical silence can mean that we can, today, make up our own minds ethically, or that we can turn to other sources of authority such as 'tradition' or 'conscience' or moral reasoning in search of an ethical directive about IVF. Or we can ask: if the Bible contains no *direct* moral authority on the practice of IVF, does it nonetheless contain *indirect* moral authority? This question leads to the second alternative.

The *second* ethical approach to the Bible apparently overcomes some of the problems of the first approach outlined above.

Although IVF, as such, is not mentioned in the Bible, and so cannot *directly* be either forbidden or permitted, there are certain *themes* or *topics* in the Bible which do relate to IVF. Examples of these are 'killing', 'adultery', 'creation', 'parenthood'. So some ethicists can still ascribe high moral authority to the Bible inasmuch as they can say that it contains topics and themes which have their source, in some way, in God and which are universally true and applicable, i.e. are not limited to particular times and places.

But on this second approach, the claim that the Bible, though it does not forbid or permit IVF, can still speak authoritatively, if indirectly, via biblical topics or themes, does become problematic. For the themes or topics do not come to us ready-patterned and packaged to serve our needs for an external, objective moral judgement about IVF. (Indeed, the biblical themes and topics are carried or borne by a huge variety of types of literature, e.g. myth, parable, history, law, saying, psalm, gospel.) Thus, we as human beings have to *bring to* the themes and topics elements of our own authority. And we use that authority to shape and pattern the themes and topics. But in this use of our own authority, different people come to very different conclusions.

The *third* ethical approach to the Bible apparently overcomes some of the problems of the first and second approaches outlined above.

Modern methods of studying and interpreting the Bible no longer make it possible to credit the *text* of the Bible with divine authority in any literalist way. Instead, it is more correct to say that the Bible *witnesses* to the complex and rich religious history of the Old and New Testament peoples, and that it is *through that history* that God is held to speak authoritatively as to what in human life is permitted and forbidden. So we, today, have to get at the substance of God's authority *via* the biblical writings which lead us in turn to that historical experience.

This approach seems to take a much more responsible attitude to what we now know about the historical contexts, origins and intentions of the biblical writings. But at the same time, because so much is demanded of *us* as agents of interpretation, we have come to recognize that, in many respects, we stand at a considerable remove from the biblical writings. It seems likely that many of our basic assumptions about the nature of human life and history and, more specifically, the assumptions we make about the nature of Christianity, about its beliefs, attitudes, and moral values, have changed appreciably over two thousand years.

In the remainder of this chapter I shall deal briefly with one scholar, and more fully with another scholar, who have both made contributions to the problems outlined above.

Flynn

A helpful point of entry is found in Eileen P. Flynn's *Human Fertilization In Vitro: A Catholic Moral Perspective*. It is, for the most part, a piece of open enquiry which does not shirk difficult questions. I am concentrating on a short section which deals with biblical 'evidence'.

Flynn describes her task as follows: 'we will look to Scripture in a heuristic way in order to ascertain the attitude which should be apparent in a Judaeo-Christian stance towards biological parenthood, and to determine if the Bible takes an explicit or implicit position on technological reproduction' ('heuristic' here means 'exploratory' or 'in a spirit of enquiry'). She observes that Scripture does not speak to the rightness or wrongness of married spouses seeking to become biological parents by IVF. But what is the significance of the Bible's silence about making an ethical ruling in this context?

She here refers to the Roman Catholic ethicist Charles Curran, who has observed that in recent Roman Catholic biblical study, the category of *law* has been relegated to a secondary role in the life of the Christian. So we should no longer seek to grasp the ethical directive primarily in terms of law and obedience to law. Thus, according to Curran, the ethical teaching of Jesus is rather understood in terms of 'conversion, agape (self-forgetting love) and discipleship'. In ethics today we emphasize the interior self over against the external act.

How one does approach the Bible is in the hope of discovering or discerning therefrom 'the posture, attitude and value system which are compatible with belief in God and Christian discipleship'. This is very different from using the Bible to provide 'proof texts' to settle disputed questions.

Given this approach, Flynn asks about the value which the Bible places on biological fertility. Barrenness, alleviated by divine intervention and reversed by the gift of offspring, is vividly presented in Genesis 21.5 (Abraham and Sarah); 25.21–22 (Isaac and Rebekah); 30.1 (Jacob and Rachel); Luke 1.5–13 (Zachariah and Elizabeth) and joyously evoked in Psalm 127.3–5. 'In Scripture children are seen not as a possession of their parents, but as a gift and blessing which bring about a relationship which provides a means for growth to all involved.' The conviction of barren women 'that fertility was a blessing from God inclines us to see in the Bible a profound endorsement for the vocation of parenthood, and an understanding of the human desire to become parents'. However, this picture 'does not provide us with a specific answer as to whether or not it is morally permissible for married spouses plagued by infertility to seek to become biological parents'. Flynn seems to be saying that the biblical passages cited above are not to be treated as proof texts; they provide, however, indications. We have to avoid any 'naive bias in favour of an unrestrained technological mindset' and, on the other hand, an 'uncritical biblical fundamentalism'.[2]

Two points may be made about Flynn's approach. First, she refers to the conviction of barren women that 'fertility was a blessing from God [which] inclines us to see in the Bible a profound endorsement for the vocation of parenthood, and an understanding of the human desire to become parents'. Flynn is clearly being cautious. Being yet more cautious, would it not be possible to say, that just as some argue today that the desire for children is a socially-constructed desire, so too the desire for children in ancient Israel was likewise socially constructed? Put in another way, Flynn does not really make out a *theological* case in which the experience of barren women in Israel is linked with a divine policy of reproduction, or with our own situation today.

The second point concerns Flynn's attitude to *donor* IVF. The relevant passage reads: 'Because of the sanctity of the institutions of marriage and the family it will be stipulated that if the procedure [of IVF] is found to be licit it should only be employed by sterile spouses who turn to it in order to become biological parents.' This passage has a very doctrinaire ring to it compared with her general outlook to IVF by husband noted above. It raises, but does not answer, the question as to whether 'marriage' and the 'family' are in fact 'time-bound' institutions as far as their place in the biblical writings are concerned. If they are such, as Flynn's subsequent analysis would imply, then the fashioning of an ethical judgement depends as much, or more, on the present-day institutions of marriage and the family. Following that route, we would then have to acknowledge the diversity of sociological forms of marriage and the family, together with their empirical character both as oppressive and creative. Further, Flynn does not make clear in what sense donor IVF is lacking in sanctity — which the passage implies.

Simmons

I turn now to explore parts of Paul D. Simmons, *Birth and Death: Bioethical Decision-Making*.[3] This has proved an influential and popular book. I will draw mainly upon chapters 2 and 5.

In chapter 1, the author defines his purposes. 'The purpose of this study is to deal with that question [what ought to be done?] in the light of the biblical revelation.' 'Another purpose of this study is to examine the question of method in using the Bible to deal with issues in bioethics.' 'This book, then, attempts to bridge the world of thought from the biblical revelation to that of medical science.' To these ends 'the meaning of biblical authority is examined, various approaches to the Bible are explored, principles of interpretation are set forth, and the ways in which specific guidance is given are indicated'.

Simmons straightaway indicates what the Bible has to offer. The Bible is without rival in the three functions of 'providing direction', 'establishing perspectives' and of 'developing norms for action'. These functions are broadly conceived and are not specific to bioethics. Simmons then undertakes to *explore* the meaning of biblical authority for bioethical decision-making.

One limitation on the Bible's authority is the lack of material in the Bible on medical science. But this is not so surprising, for the Bible's purpose is 'to deal with human issues in the light of the revelation of God'. More fully, 'the Bible is the product of God's revealing and redemptive history in the midst of the historical circumstances of people attempting to understand and do his will'.

Simmons is quite clear that there is a difference between biblical ethics and Christian ethics. He defines Christian ethics thus: '[it is] the critical and analytical study of the nature of Christian faith for the purpose of articulating the types of attitudes, conduct, and actions that are appropriate to and consistent with a life commitment to God as revealed in Jesus Christ.' The very many modes of ethical reasoning surely point to basic differences of approach. There is no *one* ethics; there are many variable factors. Simmons then makes some crucial statements to which I shall return later. 'The Bible shapes, and our interpretation of the Bible is shaped by, certain variables [my punctuation]. *One never simply uses the Bible to answer any moral question.* Rather, the Bible is read through a number of "filters" that determine what is "heard" when the passage is read. *How* one reads the Bible determines to a large degree *what* one reads from the Bible. Because assumptions and postures involved are so different . . . the conclusions drawn from and supported by the Bible are quite different.'

The first approach is *prescriptive*. The Bible 'is a source of moral rules or laws which are given for the faithful as they confront issues' in, for example, bioethics. Doing the will of God consists in obeying the moral laws which are contained in the Bible. These rules of behaviour are of universal application. In this mode of moral reasoning a rule is sought which will 'fit' the ethical dilemma at issue.

Simmons raises a number of searching questions about this first approach. For example, those who subscribe to the prescriptive view hold that: (1) revelation refers to the giving of objective doctrinal and moral truths, recorded in the Bible, about God and God's will. Those who wrote down these directly-given truths did not have to interpret what God is saying; (2) revelation is 'closed'. The Bible is God's final word to us. Nor were these writers in any way limited by the fact that they belonged to a particular culture; (3) the contemporary follower of this kind of ethics is not expected to engage in intelligent discrimination, but only to offer *immediate obedience*; (4) this kind of approach implies a military or judicial image of authority. The definition of human responsibility means — obey the rule or the law! Plainly, Simmons is not sympathetic to this first approach.

The second approach is *deliberative*. 'It attempts to discover the universally valid but general principles set forth in Scripture.' The task here is not to discover the laws or rules of the Bible, but rather those principles which lie behind the commandments. 'The principle is always morally binding, while the rule may not be.' Again, as in the prescriptive approach, there is a great variety of approaches to be found. A particularly sensitive example is that of Barnette. It proceeds by looking behind the specific laws or rules at the moral principles which are universal. Example 1: the biblical law forbidding the taking of God's name in vain expresses the principle of reverence for God in all deeds and words. Example 2: the biblical law which condemns murder expresses the universal principle of the sacredness of human personality.

Simmons finds positive features in this approach by way of principles: (1) it enables us to construct biblical perspectives on current issues which are not found in the Bible; (2) the concept of faith is handled in an interesting way which connects up with the central theme of the next chapter. Faith is not essentially about believing doctrines nor about obedience to rules. It relates more to the *exercising of responsibility to use one's intelligence to discern God's will and make creative moral decisions.*

The model of the Christian life implied by the deliberative approach therefore is one that stresses the person as a decision-maker using all the rational and spiritual resources at one's disposal. Responsibility is defined in terms of one's ability to think through a problem. Through that process the believer comes to a decision and acts upon what is thought to be right. Here the place and importance of human reason are underscored and brought under the scope of *moral responsibility.*

The third approach is *relational*: (1) the relational or responsive style 'stresses the response in faith which the believer is to make to the living presence of God'. Imitating the moral directives in the Bible is not authentic. The only behaviour which is authentic is that which arises from our response to the divine activity; (2) so, neither the person who gives unthinking, unreflective obedience to rules, nor the person who engages problems with cool, detached reflection, but the person who responds, is needful.

Simmons deals with objections

Simmons describes the 'interventionist strategies to by-pass infertility' and then considers the objections to them, going on to offer his counter-objections. His response particularly draws upon the relational model noted above.

1. AI and IVF depend upon masturbation to provide the woman with sperm from husband or donor. The classical text to sup-

port a ban on masturbation is the Onan story in Genesis 38. Onan was instructed by God to impregnate his dead brother's wife Tamar to ensure issue for his brother. Onan refused and then spilled his seed on the ground. Thus Onan's sin was not masturbation but his unwillingness to impregnate his brother's wife.

Simmons's own response is eirenic: 'Certainly, whatever moral reservations one may hold regarding masturbation, this text [Genesis 38] is not a sufficient ground to condemn artificial insemination procedure.' '. . . the intention to produce a child or to contribute to that end removes such acts [of masturbation] from the obsessive-compulsive syndrome of harmful autosexuality.'

2. Demystification of sex. Some fear that IVF, for example, will demystify or deromanticize human sexuality. Simmons responds: much of the romantic aura of sex is in fact to be ascribed to ignorance. 'Technical intervention can serve to bless us and not curse us by enabling us to better control our procreative powers and facilitate planned parenthood.'

3. Some of those concerned about overpopulation object to the NRTs because they by-pass a natural check on population growth. Simmons counter objects that very few couples will be affected by these procedures and so they will make little difference to the legitimate concern about overpopulation.

4. On the one hand Simmons paints an alarming picture of commercialization, of one kind or another, in the 'baby market'. Clearly he does not think that this is a good reason for rendering some of the procedures illegal. Instead, he relies upon measures such as 'public policy should prohibit couples from selling a child for mercenary motives . . .'. 'New legal measures will need to be developed.' The 'problem [of mercenary motives and commercial exploitation] needs to be rectified in the medical community as well as in the black market'.

5. One of the main objections to IVF relates, for many people, to the human status of the embryo. This affects, for example, embryo research, freezing, and killing of embryos excess to

need for IVF.

Simmons replies with the notion of 'anticipatory person-hood'. This is not to be confused with actual personhood. 'The fetus is not a person but should be regarded as such.' Simmons then argues that 'attributing personhood to the fetus is a func-tion of the humanity of the parents and others involved who are in fact persons'. (This is similar to my own argument set out on p. 89 below.) In fact, Simmons apparently holds that the foetus is not a baby (and therefore not a human person) until birth. It is noteworthy that he uses biblical texts to sup-port the notion of anticipatory personhood which are used by other ethicists to claim that the embryo/foetus *is* a human person (e.g. Jeremiah 1.5a).

6. Under the title of 'prospective caring', Simmons notes, among other things, that concern for the child-to-be will also weigh in the scale the psychological impact of certain procedures upon the child. An example of this revolves around the IVF or AI donor child who may be curious about his/her donor parent. Simmons replies that 'this does not seem to pose a major problem, however, and thus should not be used to condemn such procedures. It does focus the responsibility for concern at this level.'

7. It seems that Simmons's treatment of 'Procreation: the biblical promise' is a reply to the argument that IVF is illicit because it separates the unitive and the procreational. Using Genesis, Simmons claims that the creation of differentiation and the experience of sexual desire were both recognized as prior to childbearing (see Genesis 2.8 etc.). So 'coitus is not primarily for procreation but for the expression of intimate love in the context of marital commitments'.

8. God promises offspring. But this requires a distinction between the promise of procreation and the command to procreate (Genesis 1.28). According to Simmons, 'the context of the story indicates' not that you *must* have offspring, though you *may*. Thus celibates, if the latter be correct, are not guilty of disobeying a divine command.

9. Some object to IVF on the ground that it is a 'managed pregnancy'. Simmons replies that 'a child is not just another gift or a medical corrective to a physical limitation. A child is a unique gift, comparable to no prosthesis whatever' (prosthesis refers to any artificial device that is attached to the body as an aid).

10. In the Conclusion to the chapter on 'The Bible and biotechnical parenting', Simmons refers, not for the first time, to 'biblical principles'. I shall refer to this usage in my comments on Simmons which follow.

Comments on Simmons

Simmons's approach to IVF and the Bible is in fact more extensive, more detailed, and more vulnerable than that of Flynn. If the word 'Bible' were not referred to so frequently, the reader would not be unduly surprised. In the key chapters which relate to bioethics in general and IVF in particular, the amount and range of the appeal to the Bible is quite small. In the book as a whole, Genesis supplies the greatest number of citations, with Matthew's gospel second. The usage 'biblical principles' occurs frequently, though it is never quite clear what this usage *means*, and from where, and by what paths, these principles relate to the Bible. For example, if the context is rightly understood, the statement 'the love of the couple may be served by their deliberate choice to become parents' is one such biblical principle. This may correlate with Simmons's remarks about Sarah and Rachel that 'bearing a child was an important factor in their marriage and in their sense of personal fulfilment'. Simmons is already fully aware that not everything here is altogether straightforward. He writes:

> Such Biblical paradigms certainly do not establish the moral acceptability of biotechnical reproductive procedures. They do indicate how important childbearing was to the Biblical family, however. So strong was this desire that creative options were employed to bypass the frustration of sterility. *On this basis the principle can be established that infertility as such was not regarded as the will of God which must be passively accepted.*

But I have already pointed to a number of points in the text where the author has prepared a defence against possible objections of the above kind. For Simmons, a principle is not a divine command. This becomes clear in the marked preference which Simmons showed for the deliberative and relational approaches, over against the prescriptive approach, to which I drew attention earlier in this chapter. Again Simmons was very careful to distinguish in which senses the Bible was unrivalled. These were 'for providing direction, establishing perspectives, and developing norms for action'. Obviously, compared with, for example, some kinds of fundamentalism, these three roles will appear hopelessly tentative and vague. But in Simmons's use they have a definite and deliberate role to play. They are not the product of hazy thinking or careless expression. In particular, they correlate with Simmons's emphasis upon 'responsibility'. I quote the fundamental statement by Simmons in this regard:

> Faith is neither a matter of believing doctrines for which there are no rational bases nor a matter of rote obedience to rules or laws. Even though people are sinners, God gave them minds and the responsibility for using their intelligence to discern his will and make creative moral decisions.

In this context, responsibility is mainly reflective and rational. But in Simmons's answers to his objectors, it was clear that the meaning of responsibility was also concerned with taking charge of a negative situation and responding to it. It is because Simmons really believes that human beings have the capacity to act in this way that the common objections to IVF come across, in Simmons's treatment, as much less severe than they usually do in the hands of the critics.

Finally, I want to draw attention to the distinction which Simmons draws between biblical ethics and Christian ethics. At an earlier stage Simmons's definition of Christian ethics was cited:

> ... the critical and analytical study of the nature of Christian faith for the purpose of articulating the types of attitudes, conduct, and actions that are appropriate to and consistent with a life commitment to God as revealed in Jesus Christ. This involves a study of the nature of persons as moral creatures, the process of moral decision-making, the sources

of value, standards of conduct, and the goals or objectives
of the Christian life.

Thus understood, Christian ethics is a normative (i.e. expressing
value judgements as against simply stating facts) discipline, in
which biblical ethics has a role to play. Bioethical issues, and
in our case specifically IVF, form the agenda to be addressed. The
Bible, along with other sources, 'helps to provide the framework
or perspective from which they are addressed'. We have already
seen how, at certain points, in the two chapters with which we
have been especially concerned, Simmons's biblical ethics spills
over into Christian ethics as an ethics of responsibility.

It is with an ethics and theology of responsibility, affecting IVF
in particular, that the next chapter will deal.

8

IVF:
towards responsibility

In this short chapter, I want to give provisional notice about the *kind* of theological and ethical conclusions which I will be setting out in my Conclusion.

It has been deliberate policy not to begin this book with a prior statement about the theological and ethical methods to be employed. Instead I was eager to present in the early chapters some material about IVF without imposing a theological or doctrinal framework upon it.

Similarly, I wanted to provide, on a fairly broad canvas, considerations about natural law, the Bible, and other resources before these were related to the particularities of IVF.

The intention is to avoid squeezing theology and ethics into a private and limited world of bioethics — as that world sometimes seems to be in some quarters — but to expose theology and ethics to the judgement of a wider world. For both theology and ethics are, in their own way, multi-factorial disciplines drawing upon the natural and human sciences, and many sectors of experience, as well as on the more traditional sources of the Bible and ensuing tradition. But it is not a matter of somehow adding all this material together; rather our task is to help the elements to interact upon each other, creating new constellations of insight.

At the same time, because Christianity is an historical religion and because the figure of Christ in his person, teaching, agency, death and resurrection is central to the New Testament and to later history, we are obliged, whatever way we want to develop theology and ethics in relation to IVF, seriously to *maintain that centrality.*

Given all this, I shall have in mind, over the next chapters, the wider-world concept of *responsibility* which I contend is also a concept which does profound justice to the centrality of Christ mentioned in the last paragraph. It also contrasts very sharply with the ethics of *obedience*.

The document of the Second Vatican Council, *Gaudium et Spes* sees responsibility as a recent arrival in the evolution of humankind. 'We are witnesses of the birth of a new humanism, one in which women and men are defined by her or his responsibility towards their brothers and sisters and toward history.'[1] Responsibility is, first of all, about 'lived life', and about venturesome and yet deliberate action.

Responsibility's habitat is in this kind of history. So God, viewed from the standpoint of responsibility, is not a distant supernatural being exacting 'spiritual' obedience. There is no place for an otherworldly ethics running parallel to and above the ethics of this world. 'Human morality exists precisely to foster the common good, and the human good is the creation and protection of human personality.'[2]

This outlook should be compared with Hans Jonas's characterization, in *The Imperative of Responsibility*, of the earlier ethics:

> The effective range of action was small, the time span of foresight, goal-setting, and accountability was short, control of circumstances limited. Proper conduct had its immediate criteria and also immediate consummation. The long run of consequences beyond was left to chance, fate, or providence.[3]

What I am calling the theology and ethics of responsibility has nothing in common with that description.

Responsible action refers, therefore, to action which does *not* take place for the most part in systematic and uniform patterns, but rather in a diversity of contexts and often in unexpected conditions. Responsible action does not come to situations with complete answers. But, in practice, 'many traditional images of man [*sic*] as decision-maker seem to imply that the decision is a simple yes or no, uttered in the presence of definite alternatives'. 'The image of the responsible man [*sic*] as decision-maker brings into view an aspect of moral choice, which the traditional ethics either neglects or de-emphasizes.' Responsibility 'concentrates on the confusion and on the creativity of moral decision'. But responsible men or women are aware that the community's experience and their own are 'unfinished and often deceptive'. Their moral creativity is more that of the apprentice than that of the expert.

This approach is apt and appropriate in respect of the developments explored in this book. For the danger is that we shall convert these opportunities into being determined and judged by past-centred norms.

9

Some
IVF participants

So dominant has the embryo-foetus become in many ethical presentations of IVF that other important *dramatis personae* have often faded into relative invisibility. *This chapter looks at some of these other agents in their own right and in relation to each other.* The coverage cannot be complete; but these few samples might encourage the reader to identify other agents and to explore their status and roles.

The counsellor

In IVF, the counsellor has often been a hidden figure, or has sometimes been identical with the doctor — or has in fact been non-existent! I shall deal with two phases in which the services of a counsellor are vital. The first phase concerns preventative and primary counselling. (Strictly speaking, this is not directly relevant to IVF. Indeed, if successful, it would go some of the way to putting IVF out of business. But it would be irresponsible not to mention it at this stage.) There is urgent and widespread need for women and men to be able to anticipate later acute difficulties by very early advice which may be as much psychological as physical. Obviously it is also the case that the earlier that problems are exposed, the greater is the possibility of overcoming them altogether. However, as the brief case histories in Chapter 3 indicated, in some cases all measures fail and access to IVF is initiated as a last resort.

More immediately concerned with IVF is the second phase of counselling which I shall mention. The Warnock Report put it thus:

A second issue concerns the counselling, advice, information and discussion that should be available for those who seek treatment for infertility. Many of the problems which may arise in the course of treatment, whether this treatment ends in the birth of a child or not, are complex and they need to be given careful consideration over a period of time. We therefore believe that counselling should be available for infertile couples and for donors. In particular the task of the doctor and the counsellor must be to ensure that couples and donors fully understand the implications of the journey upon which they are embarking, what rights and duties they have, and where they may expect to experience difficulties. The counselling that we envisage is essentially non-directive. It is aimed at helping individuals to understand their situation and to make their own decisions about what steps should be taken next. Counselling need not necessarily take place at the hospital, though this may be the most convenient location. It should be carried out in a neutral atmosphere and involve a skilled, fully trained counsellor.[1]

This is an important statement which affects very closely the ethics of informed consent. As such, it relates also to the broader ethical criterion of autonomy. A number of points must be made.

The combination, in the above passage, of 'counselling', 'advice', 'information', 'discussion' and 'non-directive' is confused and confusing. For example, 'advice' and 'non-directive' are incompatible. A process such as the following may clarify the issues at stake.

A preliminary encounter with a counsellor will be by no means primarily medical. It will help the partners to clarify the process which has brought them to this point, their feelings about their infertility and about each other, and the alternatives open to them. It is preferable not to have this encounter in a hospital, which will medicalize the encounter at too early a stage. The partners would be *required* not to make a decision there and then, but to return for a subsequent encounter. This spacing quite often enables the partners to make a good decision not to go ahead with IVF, but to work out a positive alternative.

A rather different task would be prescribed for the counsellor once the IVF treatment has begun. The counsellor would be available to the partners after each phase of the IVF treatment, helping them to interpret their feelings and acting as interpreter between

IVF medical staff and the IVF patients. In this connection a most important matter deserves comment. Pastoral *follow up* of IVF partners is, on a number of counts, essential. It can appropriately be undertaken by the same counsellor. Closely related to pastoral follow-up is research follow-up. It is imperative that the ethical responsibility to respond to the many-sided investment put into IVF is both recognized and acted upon.

The third party in consent

It is widely allowed today that the chances of a satisfactory administration of informed consent is most likely to be achieved when there is a third party present. There is no need to specify the identity of this third party. It is essential that the third party is seen *not* to be professionally part of the IVF staff team.

Women and informed consent

Looked at from the standpoint of the woman, or woman and partner, it is essential that the administration of informed consent does not come across as simply routine or as merely self-protective for the IVF staff. It would hardly be denied that women often experience intense pressure to undertake IVF. That pressure can come from the partner, would-be grandparents, from female friends, from a commercial market with a huge turnover relating to all sorts of goods to attract the would-be or actual mother, and from a general natalist climate which is difficult to characterize, but which is nonetheless experienced as very real. It is, therefore, part of the ethics of responsibility that the other side of the picture is truly comprehended.

Women and male infertility

The second ethical topic under the heading of 'Women' which I want to consider concerns IVF and *male* infertility. Originally IVF was introduced to circumvent blocked or absent Fallopian tubes of infertile women. It is since about 1984 often a preferred choice of treatment for male infertility where there is low sperm count, poor sperm motility, or misshapen sperm. Lorber calls it a 'patriarchal bargain'.[2] To try and have a child in these circumstances, the woman has to go through the entire IVF process; the man simply provides sperm when requested.

For the woman to act in this way may be an expression of the gift-relationship towards the partner whom she loves. But it must be made clear that more is at stake than the donation of eggs, though that can often be a difficult undertaking. Indeed, IVF with an infertile male partner may seem similar, in seriousness, to the donation of, say, a kidney. But the parallel is not exact. A kidney donation may save a life; whereas IVF for male infertility may bring about a life.

In addition, it has to be asked why IVF as treatment for male infertility has come to be more popular since it is not the only option. The answer to this may be that 'the use of IVF for male infertility was attractive not only because it seemed to be a break-through for that specific problem, but because it was the only area that offered a chance to move ahead technologically'[2] with IVF. In other words, the conclusion was being reached that per-haps failures of fertilization and poor outcome of embryo transfer were significantly the product of sperm anomalies.

In the background there appear — if (say) kidney donation is at all a guide — to be signs of *gender* differences about donation. The 'male is more likely to question whether he wants to make the sacrifice' of a donation. Does the woman see donation to be a 'simple extension of her usual family obligations'? In the male, 'there is no life experience or expectation like childbirth which prepares him for this act of donation'.[2] In a more general way, men have welcomed IVF for male infertility because male infer-tility strongly stigmatizes men. So, with the use of IVF for male infertility, the burden of childlessness falls *un*evenly on the two genders. The ethical burden of responsibility is not shared.

The female partner of the male donor

A third ethical issue concerning women in IVF relates to one person in the IVF transaction who is rarely noticed, namely the female partner of the male donor. She is a shadowy figure. Her partner may have made sperm donations before and/or after their relationship began. The female partner may or may not be aware of this. If she is aware of it, she may feel herself emotionally vulnerable to events and relationships which she does not fully understand. Not least because of the anonymity usually required of the donor, there is much scope for intentional and unintentional misunderstanding. Later in this chapter there will be cause to mention the French DI scheme CECOS (Centre d'Étude et de Conservation du sperme humain) in some detail. In the present context, reference is only made to the feature whereby the donation, in the CECOS scheme, is made by the partners who, in one account, must be under 50 years of age and who must have at least one 'normal' child. The female partner is required to give her consent. Thus the donation is in a certain sense joint.

Women as egg donors

A fourth ethical issue concerning women in IVF once more relates to a woman other than the one who is seeking a child by IVF, namely an egg (or ovum) donor. This procedure sets out to help a female partner who cannot herself produce an egg. There are different scenarios for the involvement of the egg donor. For example, when a woman is undergoing infertility treatment and a number of eggs have been extracted for subsequent fertilization and transfer, she may consent to give one of the eggs to the woman who cannot produce an egg. There is no greater risk to the donor than if she were using all her eggs for her own purposes. Again, a donor may be prevailed upon to donate an egg in the context of undergoing an operation, e.g., hysterectomy. To achieve this, the operation will have to be timed to coincide with the donor's ovulation. Drug treatment may be advisable to time the ovulation with some precision. There is obviously more risk attaching to this method of donation. This is also a source for eggs which will be used for research. Given the overall shortage of eggs, it is not surprising, but no less unacceptable, that some-times undue pressure to surrender eggs is exerted on the woman who is to undergo surgery. This, if anecdotal evidence is any guide, has sometimes taken the form of promising the woman an early operation if she agrees to surrender the eggs. This form of duress is unethical. Informed consent is a very important feature of egg donation.

But, also, an ethical question of a different order arises in IVF with egg donation. This question has been ignored or treated dismissively by some commentators. O'Donovan, however, presses home the ethical point at issue:

> For the first time in the history of humanity, a woman is pregnant with a child which she did not engender. For the first time in the history of humanity children are born with three biological parents.... What *in vitro* techniques have apparently done is to divide the female role in procreation into two: the contribution of the ovum and the pregnancy.[3]

The consequence of this state of affairs, O'Donovan concludes, is that 'in the natural order we were *given to know* what a parent was.... From now on there is no knowing what a parent is.'[3]

Numerically speaking, there are two mothers. There is one ground on which this state of affairs seems immediately objectionable. Which of the two 'mothers' shall be regarded as the maternal parent? Does that have to depend on the importance which is attached to giving birth to the child over against being the genetic mother, or vice versa?

Enough has been said to make the point that IVF with egg donation is far from simply being the reverse of IVF with semen donation. That does not, however, mean to say that the two procedures are in all respects different and should in all respects be treated differently. For example, the Interim Licensing Authority, following a conference on egg donation which it had co-sponsored and at which there was a variety of views, counselled caution and reaffirmed its guidelines that 'egg donors should remain anonymous'.[4] The ethics of egg donation depend on whether one looks negatively at reproductive procedures which depart even more than other procedures from the 'natural', as pushing us yet further from biological definitions towards other kinds of definitions of parenthood. Parenthood would be recognized, as it is anthropologically, to be, not a divine norm, but a diverse product of diverse cultures.

The consultant and the disposition of embryos

I dealt at some length in Chapter 3 with the basic ethical questions about the status of the embryo. I turn now to the consultant's ethical problem of the spare or defective embryos. Though the contours of this problem have significantly changed since it

78

became technologically possible to freeze and thaw embryos. We are now in a position to use thawed embryos for return to the uterus, but there remains the question of dispensing of frozen embryos excess to need.

Since the number of eggs extracted from the ovaries relates to the number of potential embryos, it has always seemed ideal to extract all the eggs since some of them may turn out to be unsuitable for use. Sometimes it was customary to fertilize a high-ish number of embryos since, on a purely mathematical basis, the higher were the chances that some at least would survive after replacement in the uterus. But the other possible outcome was a multiple pregnancy with its high level of risk for the mother and the embryos/foetuses. The response to this situation could be selective abortion (namely the abortion of the least satisfactorily developing embryos in the uterus, with its ethical problems and clinical risks).

The Interim Licensing Authority pronounced on the number of embryos to be used as follows:

> Consideration must be given to ensuring that whilst a woman has the best chance of achieving a pregnancy the risks of a large multiple pregnancy occurring are minimised. For this reason ... no more than three ... pre-embryos should be transferred in any one cycle, unless there are exceptional clinical reasons when up to four may be replaced per cycle.[4]

Let us now suppose that five eggs are fertilized. Three embryos are returned to the uterus. Two are left behind because one is defective and one is surplus to need. It can be argued that there is no ethical objection to destroying that defective embryo by analogy with natural processes. For the high natural embryo wastage referred to above includes a substantial proportion of defective embryos, which may be 'nature's way' of seeing to it that as few of these as possible successfully implant, only to fail at a later stage. As far as the embryo in excess of need is concerned, this embryo could be frozen and used for a subsequent cycle with the same woman, or frozen and used with another woman after the first woman's consent has been given. This would require it to be possible to 'bequeath' the embryo solely for reproductive purposes, and not for research if the first woman had ethical reservations about that.

However, it could be said that the proposal made in the above paragraph for dealing with the situation is too ethically scrupulous as far as the developmentalist (or gradualist) argument about the status of the embryo is concerned. It could be argued that the good prospect for the three embryos with a view to pregnancy elicits more of our moral respect than the moral respect owing to the embryo which is in excess of need. Again, we must recall the fact that the massive 'natural' wastage of embryos in relationship to which the one embryo in excess of need in our case is numerically trivial. This is, it may be suggested, one of the contexts in which the substitution of the adjective 'natural' by the adjective 'random' is justified. Then the deliberate destruction of one or more embryos is in fact, in terms of responsibility, the 'better way' compared with random wastage.

The growing child

> The web of family relationships is far more complex than is often supposed and the implications of these relationships are far reaching.[5]

In turning now to the IVF child/adolescent/young adult, we take up the thorny and much-debated question as to what, if anything, should be communicated to the IVF child about her or his IVF status. Much has been made, in recent years, of the possible similarity, as far as this question is concerned, between IVF (and DI) and adoption. Although the similarity is not as total as some may suggest, it is a good starting-point. 'Open adoption' is now widely commended and an early proponent of this policy, Brandon, writing in 1979, explicitly explored this similarity.

In 'Telling the AID child',[6] Brandon declares herself in favour of telling the child conceived by DI, and therefore also by donor IVF, the 'unusual circumstances' of her or his conception, and that she or he had an 'earlier biological father' other than the person she or he knows as father. In arriving at this point of view, Brandon is plainly exercised first and foremost about the well-being of the child. There are other secondary considerations which will be mentioned below. Brandon's chief argument is set out as follows: we know from research in adoption that 'adopted children fare better when they are told the truth about their biological origin, provided they are told by people who care about them and how they feel and who respect their wish for factual details'.[6] Brandon makes an appeal to general experience thus: is it not true that children can very often cope with what may be harsh facts in their lives, provided they are supported by loving relationships? The reverse side of the coin, Brandon argues, is that deception of the DI child is harmful.

When it comes to the question of the donor, Brandon takes a moderate line. The degree of information about the donor to be shared with the DI recipient and her partner should be commensurate with the 'donor's right to protection and to confidentiality'. The information about the donor to be communicated with them would not go any further than, for example, a 'description of his interests, aptitudes, work, appearance and temperament'.

The picture which emerges from Brandon's brief treatment is one which would be expected from a social worker experienced in adoption. She is strongly in favour of a process for the selection which takes into account medical, social and psychological grounds. The purpose of the selection process, in its broader and narrower aspects, 'is to explore all the implications including possible hazards for the potential parents and any child conceived and to discover whether parenthood achieved through DI is right for this couple, for the recipient herself, for her partner and for any child conceived'.

Finally, Brandon makes a plea about the urgent necessity for research in the field of DI which is of such a kind as will describe the experiences of the families created, the subjective experiences of both recipient and spouse, and the development of the children. This is an absolutely necessary condition for moving towards ethically responsible decision-making in DI and donor IVF.

It will now be fruitful to examine the Warnock Report's treatment of this theme, starting as it does from a different point from Brandon. Warnock sees anonymity, for all parties, as a protection from 'legal complications' and also from 'emotional difficulties'. The legal complications refer to the genetic father being the true father of the child, leading to possibly the experience of stigma for the donor, recipient family, and DI child. If, however, the law were changed (and it has in fact been changed, Section 28 of the

1990 Human Fertilisation and Embryology Act stating that 'the other party to the marriage shall be treated as the father of the child unless it is shown that he did not consent to the placing in her of the embryo or the sperm and eggs or to her insemination') one may expect a gradual diminution of stigma and other negative responses. Warnock ventures the judgement that it does not accept that the donor is *necessarily* a threat to the stability of the conjugal relationship. A possible parallel which usually works well is that of the step-parent who is in asymmetrical relationship. But Warnock is undoubtedly exercised by another factor neither directly legal nor emotional, namely that unless a high degree of protection is afforded, donors will not volunteer. The CECOS scheme represents in certain respects an approach to DI donors which is more 'open' than other approaches. But it does not give ground on the anonymity of donors. Sweden, on the other hand, has a fairly short experience of an approach which is directly relevant to our consideration.

The abolition of anonymity in DI in Sweden led, in the first instance, to reduced participation on the part of donors, recipients and doctors. Subsequently there has been a return to the figures under the earlier legislation. The practice differs, however, in two respects: the volunteering donors are mainly older men (as in CECOS) and more of the volunteers are married (as they were required to be in CECOS). Reports comment on the success of the new arrangements. The Swedish experience may suggest that the debate on donor anonymity is on the move. Warnock concluded that, from the age of 18, basic information about the donor's ethnic origin and genetic health should be available to the child, though it did give space to describing the views of a small minority of its number, which, without compromising anonymity, commended a gradual move towards making detailed descriptions of the donor available to prospective parents. Against this point of view, it may be argued that more information on that scale cannot be reconciled with maintaining anonymity, but will rather in the long run erode anonymity.

In general, it must be questioned as to whether adoption and DI/donor IVF constitute a close comparison and, if not, which may be judged the more problematic. First, it may be argued that adoption is a response to a crisis, including the crisis of, say, the child not being wanted by her or his natural parents. Thus, being adopted may not be particularly attractive, but the crisis is there and adoption usually overcomes it. Moreover, as commonly is the case, the adoptive parents treat the child as if she or he were their own.

There are two responses to this account from the standpoint of DI/donor IVF. The first is to say that a DI/donor IVF situation is better than an adoption, because the child is a wanted child from the very beginning. This is better than not being wanted and then being wanted. (Of course it must be noted that adoption does not always arise because a child is not wanted; its parents may have died.) The second response is different. The child may say that as far as adoption is concerned, it can put up with genealogical confusion and other negative emotions. However, as far as DI/donor IVF is concerned, the child may say, as it were, that it has deliberately been brought into the world, its parents *knowing* that genealogical confusion and other negative emotions would be the consequence. They have therefore satisfied their own selfish desires by having a child in this way, without paying due regard to the plight of that child.

Either one of these two responses may be possible.

But we know from the findings of the post-1975 research on adopted children having access to data about the natural parents that a significant minority have experienced trauma of one kind and another in this unsettled state of affairs. On the other hand, some commentators have claimed that a storm has been brewed in a tea-cup and that exaggerated claims have been made about adoptees' needs and attitudes.

The best way forward, pragmatically, seems to be to treat, as far as possible, each case on its merits whilst working on the assumption that in the long run and for most children truthfulness is better than deception. In addition, it may be that the comparison with normal children is often used in an unhelpful way. Children in 'natural' circumstances have their fair share of confusion and turbulence.

The sperm donor

The sperm donor is something of a mystery man in IVF. There is a very limited amount of reliable data about IVF donors. So in this section we also draw upon DI as a source of information, though here too the data are relatively sparse, despite the fact that DI has been in use for very much longer than IVF. There is no significant difference between donor IVF and DI, so that what is learnt from DI has immediate application to donor IVF.

First, is the donor an adulterer and the IVF woman, by association, an adulteress? In the early critiques of DI, e.g., by Geoffrey Fisher, the then Archbishop of Canterbury, the charge of adultery was strongly pressed. Today, this is much less common. There may be different reasons for this change. On the one hand, it may be that the issue has been thought about more carefully and a different conclusion reached. On the other hand, with approximately 25 per cent of all children born out of wedlock, adultery may be regarded more lightly. One feature of adultery is sexual intercourse. With anonymous donors this is out of the question. Donor IVF is therefore normally not adultery. If the question is rephrased to ask whether the IVF donor possesses the motive for adultery, then that may or may not be the case. We shall have reason to note later on that a proportion of IVF donors have sexual fantasies about their anonymous or non-anonymous donor recipients. Whether or not that infringes Matthew 5.27–30, it does not constitute adultery at law. A similar account may be given of the sperm recipient's attitudes and feelings without adultery being hypothesized. But there is more to be said than this. As Jones puts it in *Manufacturing Humans*: 'may a product of someone's body jeopardize the intimacy and mutual relationships of the marriage bond? ... The element of new and future life is implicit in gamete donation, and is this, in a sense, a giving of what one "is" and "represents"?'[7]

Some ethicists have argued that the donor–child relationship is morally highly significant, as, by 'fathering' the child, the donor bears full moral and other responsibility for the child, notwithstanding his lack of personal presence to the child by virtue of his anonymity. This responsibility is inferred from the donor being the genetic father of the child. (Undoubtedly one of the reasons why donors have insisted upon anonymity has been their desire to avoid in fact taking on that responsibility. The often highly successful donor search-organizations in the USA have in that respect brought many donors to book. But the 1990 Act seems to have radically changed the situation: see above, p. 82.)

Second, the French CECOS organization, referred to above,

possesses some interesting features, some of which relate to the question of donors. One of the aims of CECOS has been to present a better public image of donation. It is central to this that the donors are not reimbursed, save, possibly, for travelling expenses. Another key policy is that donors should be married with one or more children and belong to an older age-group. (It is interesting that the English DI consultant, Mary Barton, reporting on her work in 1945, concluded that the donor should have at least two legitimate children and be 30 to 45 years old. By contrast, Curie-Cohen et al. reported on an American survey in 1979 that 62 per cent of doctors used medical students and hospital residents as donors.) An account of the Institute of Familial and Sexological Sciences at Louvain (Belgium) refers to its team (gynaecologist, andrologist, urologist, psychologist-sexologist) which interviews prospective DI recipients. The psychologist explores the motives of prospective donors and evaluates the quality and lucidity of their decision. The dominant motive among prospective donors is one of being socially helpful. They want to characterize sperm donation as a neutral physical act that, once done, is done for ever. All donors prefer to stay anonymous and strongly stress the need for discretion to avoid personal, intimate, sexual contact. This need for 'distance' possibly relates to the fear of a consanguineous marriage between their child and a DI child.

There are some negative indications among prospective donors; it is unlikely to suppose that it could be otherwise.

In one case there were neurotic feelings of inferiority after a broken relationship raised questions about X's capacity for satisfactory relationships and about the possibility of impotence, in the light of guilt feelings related to sexual identity and masturbation. Being a donor serves to provide children by way of compensation, exchanging feelings of impotence for fantasies of omnipotence.

Y is over-affected emotionally by the infertility problems among family and friends to whom he wants to give children for those that are lacking. So, by volunteering to be a donor, he lives out imaginary relationships with the donor recipients.

Huerre's small-scale study on 'Psychological aspects of semen donation'[8] at CECOS makes a few useful additional comments about donors. As stated above, a wife is required to give consent to her husband becoming a donor. 31 out of 45 couples planned to keep the donorship as a secret to family and friends, except to their own children. Nonetheless, they experienced gratification for the service which (t)he(y) would render. There was evidence of some ego-reinforcement.

At this point, it is useful to note some very brief case histories from Poyen and Alexandre concerning psychological states of male partners of women undergoing DI treatment.

U, the husband of the sperm recipient, was experiencing paranoia and was on the verge of delusions. He insisted on maintaining a constant watch on his wife at the DI premises and he included the doctors in his mistrust.

V, the husband, had suffered an acute psychotic decompensation after he was informed of his sterility, the diagnosis of which had required a month's hospitalization. The direct link could be seen through the delirious themes of persecution and paternity which he has expressed.

The symptoms, which had appeared at the moment W's sterility became known, had forced him to give up work and to stay at home. The patient insisted that his doctors make a small incision in his abdomen before they inseminated his wife, so that he could show the scar to his parents in order to prove that a surgical operation had removed his sterility.

X, married for six years, had been referred for primary sterility. Two years after the medical staff had diagnosed the condition as incurable, the couple, apparently close, reached a decision to try DI. However, one year later, Mrs X arrived in tears to tell us that her husband had just started an affair and was leaving her.

Mr Y, aged 41, had been referred because of total sexual impotence. Married at 29, he sought medical help for sterility whose congenital nature was established. Its incurability was apparently well accepted. After hesitation between adoption and DI, the latter was agreed upon. Immediately after the first insemination, sexual activity decreased progressively, ceasing totally in the weeks following the certitude of pregnancy. No intercourse took place for over two years. He seemed very attached to 'his son', now two years old, and had a strong desire for a second child. His wife is once again pregnant through DI.

What can be learnt from these case histories? First, Alexandre observes that the fact that a couple have been accepted for DI does not imply that there will be no further problems. It is important in the difficult cases to recognize that not only are the spouses to be considered, but also any DI children born into the marriage. Such an experience as DI 'cannot possibly be neutral and not upset at the unconscious level'[9] the resources of the DI couple. In a sense, for some, DI is only an event in a long pre-history and a longer post-history. But that event may signal the arrival of the DI child which has to find its way amid complex parental relations.

Furthermore, there is the question as to how the spouse of the DI woman visualizes her. Alexandre provocatively handles this issue by reference to the 'Anybody' and the 'Nobody'. He asserts that in every case — and he may well exaggerate — DI means for the woman an experience of pleasure and fertility. For the man, it means accepting being replaced by 'Nobody'. Thus separation on the initiative of the man, or impotence in the man, may be the form taken by the man's rejection of the new status of the woman fertilized by another. She is seen by the man as either 'Anybody', and thus as soiled and fit for rejection, or as 'Nobody', in which case she becomes sacred and untouchable (sc., the 'Immaculate Conception'). Alexandre has an article with the title 'On the difficulty of being St Joseph: the sterile "father" faces DI'.

All this goes to reinforce the remarks made earlier in this chapter about the importance of counselling.

Broadly speaking, the donor in IVF has not been responsibly treated and a lot of the problems associated with donors have been swept under the carpet. It sometimes seems as if the emphasis on the necessity of anonymity for donors has been made something of an excuse for not facing up to, and dealing with, the real questions about donors.

Conclusion

A wide range of agents pertinent to IVF has been considered in this chapter. By and large the analyses have shown that the ethical challenges do not lend themselves to predetermined ethical pigeon-holing. Many of the components of the ethical dilemmas are very 'situational'. Although different cases possess common features, they do not lend themselves to easy ethical generalizations. The strenuous task of working with individual cases remains. Any other way would be irresponsible.

10

IVF and embryo research

There has been a distinct difference of attitude towards the use of embryos, on the one hand, for directly helping infertile individuals and, on the other hand, for research of different kinds, though usually related to reproduction and infertility. The difference may lie in the sentiment, and sometimes sentimentality, which attaches to babies, whereas embryo research gives the impression of callousness and manipulation. It seems unlikely that many who enthused about Edwards and Steptoe's achievement knew about the number of embryos which were used and discarded worldwide to make the project of the 'test-tube baby' possible.

Many people are convinced that the primary ethical question about research and IVF is related to the status of the embryo. First of all, therefore, I shall note that the moral question arises in several contexts of IVF. Second, I examine how the question of the status of the embryo relates to these contexts. Third, I shall consider the arguments for and against research. Fourth, I shall look briefly at the 1990 Act in these connections.

The IVF contexts for research

First, in developing the technique of IVF, we must suppose that thousands of embryos were used and discarded. If the embryo is a human being, that discarding amounted to murder. We have seen earlier that Paul Ramsey was a vigorous proponent of that argument.

Second, in further improving the technique of IVF, countless embryos will be used and discarded. This is a variant of the first argument.

Third, when, after external fertilization, any embryo, otherwise destined for replacement in the uterus, is found to be defective, that embryo is discarded.

Fourth, when, after external fertilization, too many healthy embryos are available for replacement in the uterus, then some or all of these may be discarded. It is, however, not uncommon that the excess embryo(s) will be frozen and used in a subsequent replacement. But that still leaves the question of the discarding of embryos when they reach the final 'use-by' date.

Fifth, the use of embryos to research basic embryology, or to improve contraception, or to overcome miscarriage, usually involves discarding, the exception being when only observation is employed.

Sixth, in natural reproduction, there is the discarding of embryos which have been shown to be genetically or chromosomally problematic.

Views on the status of the embryo

There are three commonly-held views of the status of the embryo.

The *first* asserts that at fertilization (conception), or thereabouts, a unique individual of full human moral status comes into being.

The *second* view asserts that the emergence of the individual person occurs gradually, passing through many stages. There is difference of opinion as to the relative importance of these different connected stages. Some attach particular importance to the appearance of the 'primitive streak' because it is a threshold in the individuation of the embryo. Others point to the first signs of electrical activity in the brain.

The *third* view asserts that the human creature is not an individual person until it is sentient, thinking, self-conscious, aware of self as an independent being with a future, with memories and hopes, interacting with others, and mobile. This definition suggests at a minimum an infant two or three years old.

The first is a genetic definition. The second is a biological/physiological definition. The third is, for the sake of a better word, a cultural definition. Thus each of the definitions is partial.

The nature of the arguments

On what evidence is the genetic argument based? The official Roman Catholic point of view is that the genetic argument is based on scientific evidence. So any modification of the argument will come from a modification of that evidence. This is stated explicitly by the Sacred Congregation for the Doctrine of the Faith.

But there are theological considerations as well. It is not clear whether these constitute an *argument*. The context is that, going back to earliest times, some of the Christian thinkers, following the Aristotelian theory, had treated quickening as the decisive event which also signalled the entry of the soul. Penalties for abortion from this time forward in the development of the embryo/foetus became more severe. But equally there were thinkers who preferred to focus on conception as the crucial point. Given that context, a notable event was the 1854 proclamation by Pope Pius IX of the dogma of the Immaculate Conception, one of whose implications was that in the first moment of her own conception Mary possessed full personhood. An event of a different order took place in 1869 when the same Pope ruled against early as well as late abortion. This teaching was clarified over the next 30 years or so. It is no coincidence that this was a time when the number of abortions was increasing *and* that research was apparently 'confirming' the centrality of fertilization.

Thus, despite what I said earlier about the Vatican's reliance on scientific criteria, it is clear that Vatican philosopher-theologians could independently put together some considerations which were not *dependent* on scientific evidence.

It is also worthy of note that biblical arguments have been adduced which could establish or, perhaps better, confirm the human reality of embryonic life. The arguments have come from two sources, namely from the biblical renewal in the Roman Catholic Church and from Protestant Evangelicalism. They arise in the context of arguments against abortion, but serve other purposes too.

One example of the search for biblical texts which allegedly help this cause is a partial commentary on Psalm 139: 'You created every part of me; you put me together in my mother's womb. ... When my bones were being formed, carefully put together in my mother's womb, when I was growing there in secret, you knew that I was there — you saw me before I was born.'

The commentator then observes that '... Psalm 139 makes clear in some cases at least (such as this psalmist) there is a continuity of personal identity from conception to maturity'. But this goes too far. Surely the psalmist is using religious-devotional, poetic language to emphasize God's reliability and providential care in relation to humanity. The language is not factual language; it cannot prove or disprove factual claims about the embryo.[1]

The three different approaches to claims about the status of the embryo give the appearance of objective arguments competing to tell us what is actually the case about the status of the embryo. But a different *kind* of argument suggests, and the commentary which I have presented reinforces, that these different views on human personhood are in fact *acts of cultural construction* drawing upon scientific, sociological, anthropological, historical, moral, religious and other sources. These constructs are not rigid and fixed, but have their own history, as they negotiate different ethical problems and as they respond to new or revised data. Now I do not want to be misunderstood: cultural constructs are more than private, subjective hunches; they are the laboured products of communities. Austin seems to take too individualist a view when he writes that 'just which stage marks the start of a person's life is a matter of personal opinion'.[2]

Mary Seller, however, goes a part of the way in agreement with my approach.

> I do not consider the very early human embryo a human being. How do I *know* that it isn't a human being? I don't *know*, because there is no accepted definition of what constitutes a human being: rather, it is a judgement. What a human being is, or what constitutes a person, are not scientific facts but a judgement which is made after careful consideration of certain evidence which is considered important.[3]

More than once in this book, I pose the question 'Is the "natural" the best, the God-given? And is the "artificial", the constructed, undoubtedly the worst, the demonic?' It is, I think, one of the achievements of recent medical ethics and bioethics that we have begun to pause before answering those questions in the ready affirmative. Some statistics will make my point for me.

Slowly seeping into our consciousness is 'the enormous natural prenatal loss which is known to occur'. Caplan makes the point in the form that 'engaging in reproduction in the old-fashioned way results in babies only about 10–15% of the time'.[4]

Seller refers to evidence:

Of every 100 conceptions, it can now be reliably estimated that only around 20 will survive to be born. This is due largely, but not exclusively . . . to chromosome abnormalities. . . . The bulk of this pregnancy wastage occurs at the very earliest stages of pregnancy. Thus it is not possible to say that every single embryo conceived is destined to become a person. It has a much greater chance that it will die.[5]

Downie alludes to similar evidence from a different sphere:

Egg production in a female starts a few weeks after the embryo implants in the uterus, and a baby girl is born with between 400,000 and two million eggs in her ovaries. Most are never released. Normally in a lifetime about 400 will be lost in monthly menstruation. And on average only two, three, or four will end up as children.[6]

Again:

Sperm begin their life as cells in the *testes* and every minute about 50,000 of those cells divide, and turn into sperm. . . . Each ejaculation produces about one and a half teaspoons of semen which contain 100–800 million sperm. . . . When sperm are ejaculated . . . it has been estimated that only one out of every 2,000 sperm survive [in the acidic vaginal fluid].[7]

It is misleading to describe 'natural' as 'normal' and IVF as 'artificial', 'abnormal' and even 'demonic'. 'Natural' is sometimes seen to be a sphere of prodigal waste and loss. It is not beyond imagination that, with much more successful research, IVF could become more 'normal' than the 'natural'.

I shall now state and assess the arguments about research on both sides. Then I shall look at the implications of these arguments particularly as they are found in the provisions of the 1990 Human Fertilisation and Embryology Act.

The arguments against research

The chief argument 'against' is that we are concerned with a matter of absolute principle, of exceptionless rule. It may be put thus: it is always wrong to kill innocent human beings; an embryo is an innocent human being; it is always wrong to kill an embryo.

Now, we shall see in the different arguments a congruity between the view which is held of the status of the embryo and the attitude to research. In the first argument set out in the previous paragraph, we see such a congruity. We may not kill innocent human beings; an embryo is an innocent human being from the point (or process) of conception. This point of view is found in the formulation that the right to life is held to be the fundamental human right, and the taking of human life on this view is always abhorrent. To take the life of the innocent is an especial outrage. The explicit link with experimentation is found in the Vatican Instruction *Respect for Human Life*: 'No objective, even though noble in itself such as a foreseeable advantage to science, to other human beings or to society, can in any way justify experimentation on living human embryos or foetuses, whether viable or not, either inside or outside the mother's womb.'[8]

There are also more loosely worded arguments 'against' which nonetheless contain much force. For example, the Helsinki Declaration states that 'the interest of science and society should never take precedence over considerations related to the wellbeing of the subject'.[9]

The opponents of embryo research do not necessarily deny that many advantages can come from that research. In the quotation from Helsinki there are *the interests of science and society*. Again, those who are opposed to research recognize that a ban on the use of embryos may reduce the volume of not only *pure research* but also research in potentially beneficial areas such as the *detection and prevention of inherited disorders* or the *alleviation of infertility*, and that in some areas such a ban would halt research completely. However, they argue that the moral principle outweighs any such possible benefits.

On the point of a ban which would halt research completely, some argue differently in saying that animal studies, if these are licit, can yield all the same information anyway.

What may seem like a more second-order argument invokes 'informed consent'. Since it is unethical to carry out any research, harmful or otherwise, on humans *without first obtaining their informed consent*, it must be equally unacceptable to carry out research on a human embryo, which by its very nature cannot give consent. A point must be made here. It is generally held that there are circumstances in which informed consent can be given by proxy. Examples are various forms of emergency, especially unconsciousness, and severe mental defect. But these refer usually to consent to treatment rather than to research. I judge, however, that informed consent to research, by a proxy, is not totally excluded.

There are other more loosely worded arguments 'against' which can be mentioned.

A non-rational argument states that many people feel an *instinctive* opposition to research which they see as tampering with the creation of human life.

A very general case 'against' appeals to a widely used argument in biomedical ethics, namely that experiments with embryos put society on a slippery slope to even more awful possibilities.

The arguments for research

I will put the most comprehensive argument first. 'It is only to *human beings* that respect must be accorded. A human embryo cannot be thought of as a person, or even as a potential person. It is simply a collection of cells. . . . There is no reason therefore to accord these cells any protected status.'[10] However, it is widely not the case that we accord respect *only* to persons. Apart from the status of embryos, there is the question of non-human living creatures.

Most arguments 'for', 'while in no way denying that human embryos are alive . . . hold that embryos are not yet human and that if it could be decided when an embryo becomes a person, it could also be decided when it might, or might not, be permissible for research to be undertaken'.[11]

This is a difficult task. Some who are 'for' want to say that the embryo is throughout in a process of becoming. This is the gradualist or developmentalist approach. This does not assist us in determining when it might be proper not to undertake research. But most arguments 'for' believe that they can identify a threshold which is significant enough to make it possible for us to stipulate a 'before' and 'after', though they may play for safety by seeing to it that the 'before' comes earlier than is strictly necessary. An informative example of the problem is found in the debate about conception (fertilization). People popularly refer to the 'point of conception'. But conception is more a process than an event. Do we then stay with the 'process' or do we try to identify an appropriate 'sub-event'? One example will shed some light on this.

Some will point to 'syngamy' some 30 hours after the beginning of the process of fertilization. It is worthwhile pausing to comment on 'syngamy', not because it is necessarily the most convincing candidate for the crucial threshold, but because it witnesses to the nuanced judgements which have to be made and how these bear upon legitimate research. It has been customary to locate the union between sperm and egg in the moment when the sperm passes through the zona pellucida (the hard surface of the egg). But that is only the beginning: the egg then matures; the genetic material of sperm and egg condenses into chromosomes. Finally the male and female strands come together (syngamy) to form the new genotype (the genetic constitution of the new organism). This is an interesting example. The definition of syngamy allows for experimentation on an embryo to take place with the process of fertilization having already begun.

There are, however, other possible thresholds. Some may point to the appearance of two cells at some 36 hours after the beginning of fertilization. Others will point to the period six to seven days when implantation begins as the embryo enters the environment which will provide for its subsequent nurture and growth. Yet others will point to the appearance of the 'primitive streak' which over the period 15 to 18 days signals the embryo becoming individualized, or to the much later period of the development of the nervous system which indicates the onset of consciousness. (There is dispute about the timing.) Of course, in the Christian tradition considerable weight is given to the even later onset of quickening when the mother begins to feel the movements of the foetus.

But there is no consensus about 'when' the embryo becomes human. This is probably not surprising as the process is highly complex. And it *is* a process; one may not stop because one wants to get off.

Before I turn to the way in which the 1990 Act 'resolves' this problem, I want to look at a third category of argument which is rather different from the 'for' and 'against' lobbies. I will consider it in its simple form and then in its more complex form.

One writer asks how it is possible to identify a human being.

Is it a matter of finding the right genetic, biological and other criteria by which we can conclude that Z is a person? This is essentially a *rational* form of argument. Or — and this may be slightly difficult to grasp — do we identify human beings by the way in which we *feel* it is right to *treat* them? O'Donovan follows a not dissimilar route. He argues that 'we *discern persons only by love*, by discovering through interaction and commitment that this human being is irreplaceable'.[12] We know someone as a person as that person is disclosed in his or her personal relations to us. We do not rely on observational criteria such as brain activity because these cannot say anything at all to us about persons.

Research in the 1990 Act

I proceed now to see how all this works out in relation to the 1990 Act. A licence granted to pursue research on embryos means that one cannot keep or use an embryo *after the appearance of the primitive streak*. 'The primitive streak is to be taken to have appeared in an embryo not later than the end of the period of 14 days beginning with the day when the gametes (sperm and egg) are mixed, not counting any time during which the embryo is stored.' At first sight, therefore, this appears to be a straight-forward 'for' argument in which a threshold is crossed that results in the embryo becoming a human person. If this is correct, then the only criterion used is the embryo becoming an *individual* being.

But if we look back at the Warnock Report in the above context, the following key passage appears: 'Although the questions of when life or personhood begin appear to be questions of fact susceptible of straightforward answer, we hold that the answers to such questions in fact are *complex amalgams of factual and moral judgements*' (my italics).[13]

The 1990 legislation affecting embryo research is based on two arguments: first, a factual argument about an important objective change in the constitution of the embryo, namely individualiz-ation; *and*, second, a moral argument based on the perceived attitude at large that to date the crucial threshold later would contradict the widely held moral conviction, that embryos, though not becoming human persons at fertilization, are to be treated as if they were becoming such at a date not much later. It appears to me that these two arguments, factual and moral, are somehow fused into a single argument.

I proceed from here to list the kind of research which may be undertaken under the Act.

Types of research

Each project proposed for research must relate broadly to one of the following categories:

- promoting advances in the treatment of infertility;
- increasing knowledge about the causes of congenital disease;
- increasing knowledge about the causes of miscarriage;
- developing more effective techniques of contraception;
- developing methods for detecting the presence of gene or chromosome abnormalities in embryos before implantation;
- more generally for the purpose of increasing knowledge about the creation and development of embryos and enabling such knowledge to be applied.

Conclusion

I broadly share the view of Seller which was mentioned earlier in this chapter that, although we can undoubtedly have knowledge of factual matters regarding the embryo, the question of its status is not factual. It is a judgement which *we* make.

Part of the judgement made is that we owe respect to the embryo, granted what it is becoming and what it will come to be. It is not possible to work out a rational argument which makes objectively clear when, if at all, we may proceed with research, and when not. We have here a clash of value in which there is much to be said on both sides of the debate. In theological terms, we face on both flanks the question of suffering and the question of sacrifice. The short answer is that we must handle the situation as responsibly as we can, recognizing that neither the suffering nor the sacrifice will go away. I shall say something more about the meaning of *responsibility* in this context.

11

Human fertilization and embryology: Act and Authority

[This] is a turning point in medical research and in the destiny of mankind [*sic*]. Nothing like this Bill has previously been placed before Parliament. (Lord Houghton, House of Lords, 1990)

Within the 49 sections of the Human Fertilisation and Embryology Act are some of the most difficult, most intractable and fundamental moral questions of which any society becomes seized. (Morgan and Lee)

To devote a chapter of this book to the Human Fertilisation and Embryology Authority (hereafter HFEA) is not to display a penchant for bureaucracy. On the contrary, I am convinced that HFEA is the primary ethical instrument for establishing and maintaining social responsibility towards the NRTs. Before attempting to justify that conviction, I shall first briefly paint in the background to HFEA.[1]

The *Report of the Committee of Inquiry into Human Fertilisation and Embryology*, known as the Warnock Report, was published in 1984 and debated in the Houses of Parliament the same year. In 1985, 1986 and 1987 private members' bills failed to gain Parliamentary majorities. These Unborn Children (Protection) Bills would have made it an offence to create, store or use a human embryo for any purpose other than to assist a specified woman to become pregnant. At the same time, efforts were being made, in the name of control, to amend the 1967 Abortion Act in, for example, the 1988 Abortion (Amendment Bill) sponsored by David Alton. Late in 1987, the Government finally placed before Parliament the White Paper on *Human Fertilisation and*

Embryology: A Framework for Legislation. In 1990 the Human Fertilisation and Embryology Bill was approved. Between 1985 and 1991, some of the responsibilities which would be set out in the 1990 Act had been carried out by the Voluntary (later 'Interim') Licensing Authority (VLA/ILA), established by the Royal College of Obstetricians and Gynaecologists and the Medical Research Council. When the VLA began work in 1985, it was on the assumption that the Government would be formulating its Bill to enable a statutory authority to come into existence within 18 months to two years. In the event it took six years. The Human Fertilisation and Embryology Act received Royal Assent in November 1990. Members of HFEA had begun work before then with a view to HFEA taking on its full statutory responsibilities in August 1991.

The VLA/ILA had operated a voluntary licensing system for centres carrying out in-vitro fertilization and embryo research. The 1990 Act requires HFEA, in addition, to control the storage of gametes and embryos and the practice of donor insemination in all its forms. Also, HFEA has duties in respect of the inspection of centres and the maintenance of a central register of information of all treatments given, of all people born as a result of treatment, and of all donors. In greater detail, the duties may be set out as follows.

The theory and practice of HFEA[1]

The Act of 1990 has as its basic objectives:

- To provide a statutory framework for the control and supervision of research involving human embryos. Such research is permitted only under licence from the new statutory body, the Human Fertilisation and Embryology Authority (HFEA). HFEA may issue a licence for research which is valid only for a maximum of three years. A research licence may permit the creation of embryos in vitro and their use for specified projects, where HFEA regards this research as necessary or desirable. The projects must fall within the following aims: promotion of advances in the treatment of infertility; increasing knowledge about the causes of congenital disease and miscarriages; development of more effective techniques of contraception; and development of methods for detecting the presence or absence of gene or chromosome abnormalities before the implantation of an embryo.

- To provide for the supervision and licensing of certain types of assisted conception practice, namely those which involve the creation of a human embryo outside the body, or partly inside and partly outside, and any treatment service which involves the use of donated eggs and sperm or donated embryos. Such practices are permitted with a treatment licence from HFEA issued for a maximum period of five years. A treatment licence may authorize: the creation of embryos in vitro; keeping embryos; using sperm and eggs; testing the condition of the embryo for replacement; placing an embryo into a woman; using a 'hamster test' to determine the potency and normality of human sperm. (A licence for treatments using husband/partner sperm is not required.)
- HFEA may, in addition, issue a storage licence which permits the storage of sperm, eggs and embryos. It is issued only for a maximum period of five years.
- To effect changes to the 1967 Abortion Act, e.g. most lawful abortions must now be performed within 24 weeks.

The Secretary of State for Health: appoints members of HFEA of whom there are 21 at present, though that number is not fixed (neither the Chairman (*sic*) nor the Deputy Chairman (*sic*) may be medical practitioners, nor may they be involved in any capacity with treatment or research, though between one-third and one-half of the other members *should* be medical practitioners or otherwise involved in such activities); must approve the Code of Practice; approves the fee structure for licences; and presents to Parliament an annual report of HFEA's activities over the last twelve months and proposed activities over the next twelve months.

HFEA is required to keep under review information about: embryos; the provision of treatment services; certain prohibited activities; and the subsequent development of embryos. This last item seems to involve the collection and collation of information about the provision of abortion services for a future statutory review as provided for in the 1967 Abortion Act.

HFEA is also required to publicize the services which the

Authority provides and those which licensed centres provide; give advice and information to centres where appropriate; it publishes a Code of Practice giving guidance to centres on how they should carry out licensed activities; and gives information and advice to donors and prospective donors, to people seeking treatment or storage, or to people considering whether to do so.

Compared with the VLA/ILA, the terms of reference of HFEA are more numerous and more varied.

The Authority is structured into five committees: licensing and fees; Code of Practice, information; organization and finance; social and ethical issues.

The working of HFEA can be monitored in four ways: through the licensing committees and their functioning, and through the annual inspections of licensed premises; through the annual report to Parliament; through the powers in the Act, for the Secretary of State to make changes by way of regulations (differing types of Parliamentary scrutiny sometimes being required); and through the monitoring of finance, e.g., in the Comptroller and Auditor General's audit.

The VLA/ILA had published a Code of Practice, intended for the most part to give guidance to centres. Parts of the Code proved to be controversial. It is instructive to note some of the *issues of concern* to VLA/ILA as its period of activity came to an end: small IVF centres with inadequate facilities and staffing, and small numbers of cycles being performed leading to limited experience; very limited access to infertility treatment on the National Health Service; limited training available, especially for embryologists, counsellors, and co-ordinators; need for accessible patient information leaflets and consent forms; method of citation of success rates; needs of ethnic minorities for appropriate sperm; limit on the number of offspring born from one donor; transportation of pre-embryos outside the UK; the involvement of pharmaceutical companies in the running of assisted reproduction clinics.

The Code of Practice published by HFEA fulfils its role under the 1990 Act by 'giving guidance about the proper conduct of the licensed activities'. The eleven parts are concerned with: staff; facilities; assessing clients, donors and the welfare of the child; information; consent; counselling; use of gametes and embryos; storage and handling of gametes and embryos; research; records; and complaints. Although the Code is, as its name indicates, concerned with *practice*, it is not confined to bare functions. I come back to the Code below.

Of exceptional importance for the ethical dimension of HFEA is the Committee on Social and Ethical Issues. I shall return later to a consideration of the Committee's *ethical* method. At this point, however, I draw attention to the important issues selected, and as set out in the 1992 Annual Report of HFEA. These are: payments for gamete donors; sex preselection of embryos; donor anonymity; surrogacy; and use in research of foetal and other human tissue. The 1993 Annual Report 'reported back' as follows:

- research using foetal tissue = public consultation document planned;
- sex preselection of embryos = consultation completed and responses being analysed;
- surrogacy services not to be used by women who are able to carry a baby = inserted in Guidelines;
- a further topic, namely cloning, was 'reported back' = under consideration.

Items noted in the 1993 Annual Report as 'Issues for the Coming Year' were:

- treatment for post-menopausal women = coming under consideration;
- payment to gamete donors = coming under consideration;
- supply of semen donors = results of survey awaited;
- use of foetal ovarian tissue = consultation document to be distributed;
- information for patients and potential patients = coming under consideration and possible consultation;
- the provision of GIFT (gamete intrafallopian transfer) = coming under consideration;
- transport IVF (preparation at satellite unit, and fertilization at licensed centre) = control system under formalization = guidance will follow;
- storage of sperm and embryos = coming under consideration, leading to guidelines.

Given this impressionistic account of the 1990 Act, and of

HFEA with its principal modes of working, it is appropriate to turn now to the ethics of responsibility implied. One significant note of caution is, first of all, in order.

Morgan and Lee want to emphasize strongly that the 1990 Bill and the 1990 Act are progeny of the Warnock Report: 'The Act is a Warnock Act.' 'This is true not only in its following the report of the Warnock Committee, but also in the more important sense that the science in question is that of 1984, updated in an ad hoc and piecemeal way.' The Act 'brought before Parliament the issues surveyed by the Warnock Committee Report...'. Morgan and Lee underscore what they judge to be the essential provisionality of the achievement of 1990–91. 'It would be idle to suppose that the form in which the Act is framed will represent anything more than a temporary statement on the morality of the issues under examination.' The Act 'is a transitory marker in continued moral reflection'. Again, 'the result, *for the time being*, is the creation of a statutory licensing authority...' (my italics). I am not convinced that HFEA is marked out for so short a tenure as Morgan and Lee suppose.

HFEA's medical ethics

I turn now to investigate HFEA's ethical method. It is difficult to know whether this has been deliberately contrived along the lines which I suggest or whether it has emerged less self-consciously. For the analysis which I shall present, it is not a matter of great moment to answer this question in the affirmative or the negative.

I begin with the Committee on Social and Ethical Issues' received terms of reference. The Committee was charged:

- 'to study particular *subjects* in depth...'. This is a wholesome beginning. But it is vitally necessary to determine the full scope of a 'subject' (see Conclusion).
- 'to obtain and consider the facts of each matter'. This is what ethicists have in mind when they bring together the *facts* of the *moral case*. Again we shall have to make sure what is the scope of 'the facts'.
- 'to identify the separate issues involved in each matter'. It is frequent that, in what we call 'an ethical problem', there are a

number of ethical issues. We have to tease them out and put them in some order of priority.

- 'to identify the various interests of all those involved in each matter'. These interests may, for example, be related to political, religious and social policy. Sometimes the holder of any one or more of these interests may be conscious or unconscious that she or he owns them.
- 'to consider different views in terms of argument and sentiment'. At this point classic ethical arguments may be tested out in relation to the matter in hand.
- 'to work towards a steady and general point of view . . . based on moral reasoning'.

I shall delay commenting on the ethical dimensions of these terms of reference until I have discussed another important body of HFEA material — *much* more important than it may at first sight seem — this time drawn from the Introduction to the Code of Practice.

'In framing it [the Code of Practice], we have been guided both by the requirements of the Human Fertilisation and Embryology Act and by [four considerations]:

- *the respect which is due to human life at all stages in its development;*
- *the right of people who are or may be infertile to the proper consideration of their request for treatment;*
- *a concern for the welfare of children, which cannot always be adequately protected by concern for the interests of the adults involved; and*
- *a recognition of the benefits, both to individuals and to society, which can flow from the responsible pursuit of medical and scientific knowledge.'*

We can describe these 'considerations' through a number of different filters. First, we can see them as the four main points of *contention* in, e.g., the Warnock Report and in the Human Fertilisation and Embryology Act. These four points are:

1 The status of the embryo;
2 The status of infertility;

3 The identity of children by donation and in relation to genetic therapy for the parents;

4 The question of research.

Again, these four 'considerations' can be interpreted through a filter of *compromise*. This procedure should not be summarily rejected; 'compromise' enjoys positive as well as negative meanings. The compromise works out as follows. We will not go so far as to say that at conception the resultant embryo is a personal human being in the full sense of the term, but we do undertake to treat the fertilized ovum with a degree of respect congruous with its stage of development and compatible with the respect that has to be paid to other participants in assisted reproduction. Respect is also to be accorded to women and men 'who are or may be infertile'. They are entitled to 'proper consideration' if they request infertility 'treatment'.

Much depends here on the definition of 'proper consideration'. Does 'proper' also imply 'improper' and so exclude certain categories of person from claims upon the embryo? Respect is to be shown to children. The right of adults to receive 'proper attention' may be qualified by the parallel right of children to protection. Respect is also to be accorded to the undertaking of research. But this is limited, given the other rights to be exercised, to areas which stand in close relationship to matters of reproduction.

Critique of HFEA's medical ethics

I hope that I have already conveyed that the main HFEA documentation, i.e. the Annual Report and Code of Practice, yield an impressive beginning to HFEA's reflection on many and varied issues that have fallen upon its desk at a very early stage. I have also drawn some attention at least to the initial signs of HFEA's reflection upon its reflection. The criticisms which I will make are intended to be sympathetic in the sense that HFEA is going in the broadly correct direction as far as its medical ethics are concerned.

First, methodologically HFEA has moved straightaway to an ethics defined by its own task, i.e. infertility treatment and related research. This is clear from the observation that, in framing the Code, it has been 'guided both by the requirements of the Human Fertilisation and Embryology Act' and by the four considerations, to which I shall shortly turn. In consequence, HFEA finds itself limited in the amount of internal critique it can generate vis-à-vis the 1990 Act. From this position, it is clear that HFEA is 'buying into' the cultural judgements espoused by the majority view from the appearance of the Warnock Report to the setting up of the Authority. Another way of putting this is to say that, in respect of the topics with which it deals, HFEA does not critically acknowledge that these come laden with presuppositions of many kinds. It stands by the 1990 Act in an uncritical way, though I am not convinced that it was obliged to do this. This leads to some particular concerns with which I shall now deal.

Second, HFEA, in common with the genre of literature to which it belongs, 'medicalizes' the topics with which it sets out to deal. I have already referred to the notion of 'medicalization' so that there is no need to repeat those comments here. It would take too much space to investigate *why* this medicalization takes place. In the limited case of HFEA, the question may be asked whether 'medicalization', for example, was the 'cause' or the 'effect' of the choice of criteria for membership of the Authority. It was probably a combination of both. Allowing that there is a little uncertainty about which camp one or two of the members belong to, the division — and the Act is very specific about the proportions of membership — is eleven persons belonging to the medical and scientific category and ten persons belonging to the 'lay' category. The question of the meaning of 'lay' membership of commissions and other like bodies is a vexed and tangled one. Usually lay members are not expert, except where experts outside the main area of expertise, e.g. lawyers, are required. Lay members have a certain representative function, viz., the person on the Clapham omnibus or the *vox populi*. I suggest that the lay function, if that term is still admissible, has somehow to refer to persons who understand the medico/scientific world-view but appreciate at the same time its cultural relativity. I am not presuming to say that the membership of the Authority lacks any such people. But the outcome, in this respect, is clearly and significantly seen in the social-ethical topics which HFEA has in hand. These are mainly medicalized in the form in which they appear.

Third, there is undeniable evidence that HFEA has not adequately taken note of the main force of the feminist material of which I give some account in Chapter 5. The 'woman' is not present in the four 'considerations', except that she may be invisibly present in the 'adults' of the third 'consideration' where the context is somewhat pejorative.

Fourth, a distinctly odd remark in the Code of Practice, referring to the four 'considerations' reads thus: 'We recognise that these considerations may sometimes conflict and have sought to reconcile them in a way which is both practicable and in accordance with the spirit and intentions of the Act.' It is surely right to say that the conflict in the 'considerations' is a conflict first and primarily experienced 'in life'. HFEA is not capable of 'reconciling' the considerations where they conflict among themselves, because they would first have to be reconciled, or endured, 'in life'. It is also worthy of mentioning that, without explaining why, a reconciliation model is preferred to a conflict model.

Fifth, the 'considerations' are very individually, rather than collectively, orientated. In Chapter 12, I explore this theme in connection with, for example, the use of power in the context of social responsibility.

Conclusion

The 1990 Act and the establishment of HFEA are tentative essays in *social* responsibility. What seem to be mere exercises in compromise and conflict ought not, in fact, to be belittled. The processes of moral reasoning begin with a commitment to establishing the facts of the case. Furthermore, there is no doubt that the choice of facts is profoundly affected by the wide range of presuppositions represented in our society. The critical question is whether it is feasible to move beyond that elementary stage of moral reasoning. A practical way of asking the crucial question focuses upon the procedures of HFEA. There is no doubt that HFEA is, and must be, an exceptionally bureaucratic body. For HFEA to fulfil its required routine functions is no small matter. So we must ask the question, by what means is HFEA enabled to give sustained thought, *which is more than reactive*, to developments of future policy?

12

The wider society

In this chapter, working from four different standpoints, I shall endeavour to situate IVF as an ethical issue in the context of the wider society. These standpoints are: the move from individual to social ethics; the relations between religion and technology; technology and political power; commodification and commercialization.

From individual to social ethics

So much of modern ethics, including moral philosophy, moral theology, Christian ethics and biblical ethics, has been focused on the decision-making of the individual in respect of moral issues which affect the individual. This gives a highly distorted account of ethics. Moreover, in turning to the social dimension of ethics, it must not be supposed that this dimension is the individual dimension writ large. Social or collective ethics has its own way of raising questions and of arriving at conclusions.

So far in this book we have, for the most part, been concerned with ethics as they relate to the individual. Some scholars use the adjective 'individual' to draw a contrast with 'social' ethics. We could use the words 'microethics' and 'macroethics' to make a not dissimilar distinction between ethics on the small scale and ethics on the large scale. But it is necessary to be cautious. Human beings are 'social beings' and so there are all sorts of connections and groupings, individual and social. Nor are the patterns of 'causation' simple and straightforward. There is instead a mêlée of causes and effects and counter effects. Now, one of the reasons for this one-sided emphasis on individual ethics has been the influence of the philosophy of 'individualism' with its stress on 'individual autonomy', particularly since the Enlightenment, but also before then. Another different kind of reason for this emphasis upon individualism is the sheer bewildering complexity and scale of macroethics. In Christian ethics too, in the West, individualism has been common and influential. It is interesting how the Ten Commandments, the Sermon on the Mount, and a good deal of St Paul's and Pauline ethics have *not* been recognized for what they are, namely community ethics. One reason for the prominence of individualism in medical, or health care, ethics has lain, for the most part, with the doctor–patient relationship, while the field of community medicine has been hived off as a separate discipline.

Furthermore, as we have seen, 'feminist ethics considers the interconnectedness of persons in society to be morally significant, in contrast to the assumption common to most of the leading Western ethical theories that persons are essentially separate, autonomous beings'.[1] For example, 'most of the mainstream discussion on abortion, for instance, has focused on the questions of moral status of the fetus and the mother's right to control her body. But a feminist ethical analysis demands that we also consider the social conditions. . . .'

There is now an increasing number of signs of the recognition of IVF in the context of the wider society. While infertile men and women who *seek* help view the ethics of IVF from a personal standpoint, many of those who *offer* help are becoming more aware of the social implications and the need for ethical guidelines.

Relations between religion and technology

The patterns of relationship between religion and technology (here medical technology and especially IVF) are complex. I shall describe some aspects of this complexity by reference to Jones and Matthews's classification[2] which looks particularly at *innovation*.

A religion may spread into a region and may encounter a technology which is novel to it. But the religion shows no awareness of, or interest in, the technology. Then there is the case of the religious tradition which accepts an established technology. On the other hand, a religious tradition may reject the use of a product of a technology (cf. the rejection of alcoholic beverages in some of the churches). The religion may be aware of the technology, but does not want to use it for its own purposes.

The same is true of inventions. Different attitudes arise towards new discoveries in societies where a religious tradition is established. The religion may be unaware of the invention, or, though aware of it, may ignore it. Or, it may be that the religion can provide the intellectual framework and dynamism needed for the use of a newly developed technology, printing being a classic example.

But, rejection of, or opposition to, a new technological device or process by a religious tradition, organization, or leader has been so common in the West since the industrial revolution that it seems a natural part of the landscape.

Cotton Mather was a third-generation American Puritan minister of religion. In 1771 he championed inoculation as a means of combating smallpox. In the process, he found himself opposed by the great majority of Boston's doctors. Mather had read in the *Philosophical Transactions* of the Royal Society that inoculation had been successfully used in China and Turkey. One of Mather's black slaves reported that the procedure was used also in Africa, that he himself had been inoculated, and that he had gained subsequent immunity for the price of a mild attack of the disease. Confronted by the epidemic of smallpox which was raging in Boston in the summer of 1771, Mather persuaded one doctor to try inoculation. The process required the transfer of infectious matter from the open sores of a smallpox victim into an incision in the person being inoculated. The doctor inoculated his son and two slaves; Mather had his own son inoculated. All survived.

The doctors who opposed Mather and the doctor, even to the extent of arguing their case before the city magistrates, used both religious and scientific arguments. Mather and the doctor experienced public abuse, arson and bombing. After the epidemic, statistics showed that 15 per cent of those who had not been inoculated, and only 2.5 per cent of those who had been inoculated, had died. An alien technology had been rejected by a religious tradition.

We also have to reckon with the indirect consequence of religion upon technology. An example is the thesis that the positive Judeo-Christian view of creation as orderly made possible in the West both the scientific and the technological manipulation of the natural order. A similar thesis is that of Max Weber who claimed, in broad terms, that the Protestant work ethic was a key causative factor in the rise of capitalism.

There is also the reverse impact, namely the effects of new

technologies upon religion. Technological innovations indirectly affect religion by providing alternative and competitive values, social institutions and belief systems, to the extent that the religious tradition suffers. Also, technological advancement fosters the development of social institutions which assume some of the social functions previously served by the Church. Again, technological society has made a great variety of activities to flourish, so that the local church has ceased to be the centre of social life. Finally, technology indirectly affects religion by offering alternative sources of authority.

What can be learned from this classification that can illuminate our understanding of the NRTs?

The first feature which deserves mention is that the patterns of relationship between technology and religion reach back into the distant past. They are not only contemporary phenomena. As McNeil observed: 'My own sense of the continuities in the history of medical and scientific interventions into reproduction make me cautious about such judgement [as that we live in a "reproductive revolution" or in "the age of biotechnology"], if that is to be taken to mean that technology is new.'[3] A better contrast is probably between slow changes in the past and much more dramatic changes in the latter half of the twentieth century, which the churches and the medical profession find difficult to handle.

Technology and political power

> Max Scheler called science 'Herrschaft-Wissenschaft', knowledge which gives dominion.[4]

At a certain point quantity becomes quality, which introduces a totally new dimension into our problem. 'If we develop an inexpensive [reproductive] technology, with an implantation success rate of 50%, or sex pre-selection rates of over 90% accuracy, then it is going to affect very many people in the world.' When a new technology becomes commercially significant, then it becomes power. 'The new technology thus becomes another way in which power expands and institutionalises itself in society.' If a cheap, easily obtainable, efficacious method of sex-selection enters the market, governments may need to intervene with the regulation of sex ratios.

Technology creates power. And the use of power, where it goes, and who exerts it, is fundamentally and finally a political problem. Every form of technological innovation . . . historically, has finally been coopted by the state. . . . As influenced by reproductive technology, the future may have distinct dystopian possibilities.

Ellul explores how, in a Christian frame, these dystopian [dystopia, i.e. a realm where everything is as bad as it can be] possibilities can be countered.[5] For Ellul, utopia is the central myth of our technological world-order. This myth makes us, as human beings, obedient to its demands: 'We will put up with any dehumanization . . . we will accept any demand for efficiency and give up any freedom, as long as we believe we shall be rewarded with utopia.' But we continue to nourish ourselves on utopian thought, seeking freedom and fulfilment, only to finish in slavery and alienation. The technology which offers us the gift of freedom and security in fact creates less freedom and more insecurity. In a technological society, every positive action has a negative reverse side. For example, a world of plenty becomes a world of pollution. So we have to say that the prospect of utopia is, at one and the same time, the prospect of apocalypse. The more that we move in the direction of utopia, the closer we come to an apocalypse of self-destruction.

What has this understanding to say about Christian ethics? Ellul argues that God as creator brings into being *both* the order of society *and* an openness to change and transformation. So there are in society two different but related modes of action, namely the political-technological mode of action and the apocalyptic mode of freedom. In other words, these two modes reveal a tension between the world (i.e. the technological ethics of efficiency) and the Gospel which cannot be reduced or reconciled. Ellul talks, instead, about 'the ethical inventiveness of Christians'. 'Ethics' means continually thinking out how to keep alive the tension between the technological society and the Gospel. If we can indeed keep that tension in operation, we may prevent the technological society from forcing its claims upon us.

We see in Matteo and Ellul, albeit in different ways, an understanding of technology which goes far beyond the basic definition of 'the practical application of scientific knowledge'. Technology means much more than technique.

Commodification and commercialization

We have seen so far in this chapter something of the contexts in which the NRTs, and IVF in particular, come to occupy *in the wider society*, over against the face-to-face encounters of individuals. First, we looked at the shift in the nature of ethics which was required to engage with the wider, public context. Second, we explored something of the long-standing history and broad scope of the complex interplay between religion and technology. Third, we examined the relation between technology and power. Every major form of technological innovation is co-opted by the state. Ellul argued that we have to keep alive the tension between technological society and the Christian Gospel so that we are not coerced by the former. Without doubt, looking from these different standpoints, there is a measure of apprehensiveness about the negative influence of technology in our society. Thus, in the final section of this chapter, it is profitable to try and see what happens when an NRT ceases to be simply a person-to-person matter, but instead becomes a phenomenon in the wider society.

Rothman says:

> We are facing the expansion of an ideology that treats people as objects, as commodities. It is an ideology that enables us to see not motherhood, not parenthood, but the creation of a commodity, a baby. We are involved now in the fixing of price tags to the separate parts of the reproductive process. We are negotiating the prices for bodily parts, bodily fluids, human services, energy and lives, as we produce 'valuable' babies, 'precious' babies.[6]

Commodification has been defined as a business transaction in which sums of money change hands. What is to prevent the extension of this business approach to the *sale* of babies whatever their mode of production? This is an example of the slippery slope in operation. So, one has to challenge the very presupposition that procreation is a business.

The practice of 'commercialization' is very close to that of commodification. Further arguments rejecting these two practices may be set out as follows.

- Some interpret the purchase of living, bodily material as putting the vendor in a position where she or he is being treated as a means to an end. This goes against the moral obligation to show respect for persons and to appreciate people as unique individuals. Blood donation is a different case. It fosters people's social solidarity by increasing responsibility towards one another. The market transaction decreases the sense of mutual responsibility.
- Some ask, in addition, what might be the consequences for women, children, families and the wider society if it is permitted that this significant and intimate sphere of life becomes commercialized. Will this, for example, lead to a category of ownership being prescribed for parents towards children, with diminution of human rights for the latter?
- Some question whether, if women's bodies or bodily parts are increasingly bought, sold or rented, women will become even more unequal with men.
- Some argue that this commercialization is objectionable because the women in question are being exploited. This is not the same as 'coercion' because the women are volunteering. But some would contest this and go on to say that it may be the women's economic need which is coercing them to volunteer. Some would argue that commercialism in this area is morally illicit even if it is not coerced or exploitative. They would say that some things just should not be commercialized.
- Some claim that the infertile couple are financially and emotionally exploited in their desperation to have a child.
- Some suppose that the IVF child's self-esteem will be damaged by the knowledge of the commercialization and commodification surrounding his or her birth.
- Some would say that the commercialization will benefit some groups in society more than others, i.e. rich more than poor, men more than women. Appeal is made to the evidence, for instance, about poor South American women being persuaded to act as contract mothers (popularly but erroneously called 'surrogate mothers') for which they are paid a pittance. The middle operators make large profits as the commissioning

parents ultimately foot a large bill. This 'trade' should not, of course, be viewed separately from the already widely and hotly discussed commercial practices of transnational corporations, and others, regarding pharmaceutical products in general.

• Some contend that today's social and economic forces have created the conditions for trade in gametes and/or embryos.

I want now, coming to the end of this chapter, to look at two different responses to the positions outlined above. When these have been considered, the moment will have arrived to investigate the question of legislation and regulation.

First, one common ethical objection to commercialism in the NRTs can be formulated by looking at its alternative. Contract motherhood is a notable example of this, but it appears in other contexts too. In the case of IVF it can apply to gamete and to embryo donation.

Raymond observes that in many state legislatures in the USA, strong legal and ethical objections have been raised against *commercial* contract motherhood arrangements. For example, in the *Baby M* case the New Jersey Supreme Court, in its appellate judgement, found surrogate contracts contrary to the law and public policy of the state. However, many have regarded *non-commercial* arrangements as legally and ethically permissible — *because they are altruistic and voluntarist.* Now, primarily, it is women who constitute the altruistic population. Raymond is eager to examine what she, in a striking phrase, calls the 'unexamined hallowing' of this altruism.[7]

Some commentators have come to the view that 'one can distinguish between doing something out of love and doing it for money'. A sister remarked: 'I know I couldn't be a surrogate mother . . . I'm doing this for love and for my sister.' A number of writers refer to the underlying theme, e.g. 'The moral expectation upon women is that they be nurturant, that is, that they ought to go beyond respecting rights and meet the needs of others'. One writer calls this 'supererogatory morality'. It attracts a feminist critique: '. . . the assumption of a special obligation to self-giving or sacrifice . . . is male-generated ideology.'

Second, 'the potential for women's exploitation is not necessarily less because no money is involved and reproductive arrangements may take place within a family setting. The family has not always been a safe place for women.' While there may be no financial inducement, there may be 'coercion of family ties' which involve, say, one sister giving to her sister what the family see as the greatest gift, namely a baby. Anthropological evidence points out that gifts fulfil certain obligations and are 'experienced as prescriptive and exacting'. Within the family it may be seen as dishonourable for the woman not to undertake the reproductive duties which the family as a whole wants. But this is only to see the question in an individual way. Raymond argues that 'on a political level it reinforces the perception and use of women as a breeder class and reinforces the gender inequality of women as a group'.[7]

It seems that some members of the legal profession, and others too, have settled too easily for the crucial matter being payment versus non-payment. We have seen that payment *may* be coercive, but that also non-payment may be coercive. It remains to be asked whether payment is *necessarily* coercive. Cannot the parallel with other people who perform a service in society, and who are paid for it, be invoked? Even in that scenario there may be coercion, inducement and other reprehensible features, but *there need not be*. In other words, there are proper forms of commercialism and improper forms of commercialism. How is responsible behaviour safeguarded in this respect? Such a question has to be directed to each of the NRTs, including IVF. But it must also be directed to the NRTs as a whole.

In this chapter we have seen that the significance of IVF has moved out far beyond the boundaries of a narrowly interpreted medical ethics. We are dealing, as far as technology, power, commodification and commercialization are concerned, with society-wide implications. It is therefore necessary to develop the concept of responsibility to take sensitive account of these changes.

13

Conclusion

Responsibility

In Chapter 8, I introduced the concept of *responsibility* into the discussion about IVF. It is a useful concept for, as well as being used in many empirical contexts, e.g. politics, social policy and criminology, it has played an important role in secular and religious ethics, and in theology, in recent times. In this last connection, I am reminded especially of the *Ethics* of Dietrich Bonhoeffer, now obscure, now illuminating, now fragmentary, reflecting the inner and outer turmoils of his prison years.

It has to be frankly admitted that in IVF and related subjects there is, ethically speaking, little that is straightforward. In one aspect or another the ethical scales seem to be balanced. The experts are constantly divided in the counsel that they give and in the judgements that they make. We have seen how, again and again, the argument has been pushed back in search of broader ethical principles which can then be applied to illuminate particular cases. To take but one example, granted that IVF is in some respects a species of technology, we might hope that, in going back to broader ethical discussions of technology and society, it will be possible to isolate some plain alternatives that can then be related to the quandaries of IVF. But, in fact, we discovered in Chapter 12 a variety of relationships between technology and society that defies easy classification and analysis.

In this Conclusion, I come to the judgement, that at first may seem rather depressing and faint-hearted, namely that *we should probably acknowledge that we are not yet in a sufficiently secure position to reach solid and confident ethical conclusions about IVF.* But this does not mean that I recommend that we should wave the ethical white flag of surrender. Nor does it necessarily mean there is any shortage — in quantity at least — of ethical thinking about artificial procreation. But I do contend that, in one essential respect at least, we are ill-prepared for that thinking.

This concerns the setting, context and environment in which the ethical debate about IVF is taking, and should take, place. Who is caught up in this debate? The IVF woman, the IVF woman's partner, the IVF woman's nuclear and extended family, the donor's partner and family; the GP, the IVF unit's staff including the counsellor; researchers into IVF and related fields, ethical committees; pressure-groups; the Human Fertilisation and Embryology Authority; Parliament.

The above listing reveals very clearly the 'medicalizing' tendencies which are dominating IVF. But first and foremost IVF is to be construed as a *human* event and as a *human* process. So, structuring IVF — and thus far this has only happened for the most part in a piecemeal way — it is important to arrive at accurate accounts of what is actually going on. Thus, responsibility has two functions, first, to clear the ground of falsely predicated attitudes and theories. Only when this is done can we responsibly take on the seeding process, so that IVF is recognized for what it is, rather than treated as a defective form of something else.

I shall develop this line of thought from three standpoints. In doing so, I shall try to be alert to the importation into the phenomenon which we call IVF of *alien categories* whose use in the context of IVF should be regarded as *irresponsible*. This kind of importation obviously undermines from the start the possibility of ethical integrity in IVF.

The first example that I shall give surrounds the use, admittedly less common than heretofore, of the term 'adultery' to describe what is going on with donation of sperm in DI and IVF donor. 'Adultery' is a term conventionally reserved for voluntary sexual intercourse between a married man or woman other than the legal spouse. In DI and IVF donor, there is no sexual intercourse. And whereas in adultery one of the principal motives is sexual pleasure, in IVF donor the principal motive is procreation. Of course, the feelings involved are more complex than that for the two people concerned. But the point being made is that an *anticipatory* accusation of adultery is both misleading and mistaken. What we know very little about is what goes on in that donor–recipient relationship, ignorance of which may hide from us future difficulties for many of those involved in IVF, not least for the IVF child. So there is, in addition to the irresponsible misuse of the word 'adultery', also the irresponsible lack of creativity and imagination in constructing this stage of the IVF as *a positive social event*, with its secular or religious liturgy. This leads to my second example.

I want, once again, to consider the question of *technology* which leads many people to draw a premature distinction between 'natural' and 'artificial' procreation. These terms are loosely used. 'Natural' is employed with the implication of a benign, healthy, natural order. But it also has an association with the concept of natural law (see Chapter 6). Thus 'nature' is related to both the 'gift' and 'command' of God. 'Artificial', on the other hand, has associations with harmful material, as in such phrases as 'no artificial colouring'. 'Artificial' also refers to that which is 'man-made', a usage which may have sexist connotations. In one theological tradition, 'man-made' may suggest the presence of hubris, of people trying to ascend to the status of God by their own powers, as was the case with those who built the Tower of Babel. In this connection technology means 'playing God' in one of the negative uses of that phrase. We should, therefore, move very gingerly in these linguistic minefields. More analysis indicates, I suggest, that we are not concerned here with a permanent antithesis between natural and technological, but rather with what is called a 'dialectical' relationship between the two, in which there is coming and going, diverging and converging, but never the one without the other. The feminist writers (see above, Chapter 5), for example, are not simply rejecting IVF technology but rather lamenting the non-dialectical nature of the person-centred and technology-centred relationship. So the theme of 'responsibility' surfaces again; all those who are involved in IVF, not only the 'technodocs', have to carry, and live out, that responsible relationship if refined ethical judgements are to be made. I draw from this second example the conclusion that IVF technology can carry a positive human function, different from, but not worse than, 'natural procreation'.

My third and last example is taken from the establishment of the Human Fertilisation and Embryology Authority to which I have already devoted a substantial amount of space. The setting-up of that body was in itself an ethical act. It has enacted important instruments of responsibility about IVF and other procedures. The two main categories of membership (see Chapter 11 above) can be interpreted as a movement in the direction of the kind of dialectical relationship which I mentioned in the preceding paragraph. But more than this is required. A glance at the list of research projects published by the Interim Licensing Authority reveals a concentration upon medico-scientific-technological research. For the reasons which I have given, this must be regarded as dangerously one-sided. *The most valuable source for ethical reflection that we have in respect of IVF is nothing less than the self-understanding, individual and corporate, of those involved in these processes from a variety of standpoints, expressing itself through collaborative undertakings, not least in IVF.* Against that criterion, the Authority is defective through the absence of persons and interests related to the human and social sciences.

Thus, IVF is all too often adversely contrasted with *normal* procreation. And the *normal* is far too swiftly identified with *Christian* norms. That settles the matter! I have argued, to the contrary, that the way forward is to let the received views of procreation and the contemporary views of IVF impact on and influence each other through responsible dialogue.

Notes

Definitions

1 M. Stanworth (ed.), *Reproductive Technologies: Gender, Motherhood and Medicine* (Oxford: Polity Press, 1987), pp. 10–11.
2 R. Arditti, R. Duelli Klein and S. Minden (eds), *Test-Tube Women: What Future for Motherhood?* (London: Pandora, 1984), p. 1.
3 R. T. Hull (ed.), *Ethical Issues in the New Reproductive Technologies* (Belmont, CA: Wadsworth Publishing Company, 1990), p. xi.
4 Stanworth, pp. 10–11.

Introduction

1 Department of Health and Social Security, *Report of the Committee of Enquiry into Human Fertilisation and Embryology* (The Warnock Report) (London: HMSO, 1984), p. 76.
2 S. Firestone, *The Dialectic of Sex: The Case for Feminist Revolution* (London: Jonathan Cape, 1971), pp. 225–33.
3 M. McNeil, I. Varcoe and S. Yearley (eds), *The New Reproductive Technologies* (Basingstoke/London: Macmillan, 1990), pp. 1–3.
4 Stanworth, p. 4.

Chapter 1 Infertility

1 S. Downie, *Babymaking: The Technology and Ethics* (London: The Bodley Head, 1988), chs 3 and 4.
2 C. R. Austin, *Human Embryos: The Debate on Assisted*

Reproduction (Oxford: Oxford University Press, 1989), p. 86.

3 S. Glazer and S. L. Cooper, *Without Child: Experiencing and Resolving Infertility* (Lexington: Lexington Books, 1988).

4 C. Crowe, 'Women want it: in vitro fertilisation and women's motivations for participation' in P. Spallone and D. Steinberg (eds), *Made to Order: The Myth of Reproductive and Genetic Progress* (Oxford: Pergamon Press, 1987), p. 90.

5 Glazer and Cooper, p. 12.

6 Crowe, p. 88.

7 Glazer and Cooper.

8 Congregation for the Doctrine of the Faith, *Instruction and Respect for Human Life in Its Origin and on the Dignity of Procreation* (London: Catholic Truth Society, 1987), *passim*.

Chapter 2 Historical moments

1 D. B. Johnston, 'The history of human infertility', *Fertility and Sterility*, 14 (1963), pp. 261ff.

2 M. Taymor, *Infertility* (New York: Grune and Stratton, 1978), pp. 3–5.

3 S. Fishel, 'Human in-vitro fertilisation and the present state of research in pre-embryonic material', *International Journal on the Unity of the Sciences*, 1 (1988), pp. 174–214.

4 A. Schellen, *Artificial Insemination in the Human* (Amsterdam/Houston/London/New York: Elsevier Publishing Co., 1957), pp. 7–24, esp. pp. 19ff.

5 M. Barton, K. Walker and B. Weisner, 'Artificial insemination', *British Medical Journal* (January 1945), pp. 40–3.

Chapter 3 The IVF process and its ethical problems

1 J. Lasker and S. Borg, *In Search of Parenthood: Coping with Infertility and High-Tech Conception* (Boston: Beacon Press, 1987), pp. 51–2.

2 S. Williams, 'No relief until the end: the physical and emotional costs of in vitro fertilisation' in C. Overall (ed.), *The Future of Human Reproduction* (Toronto: The Women's Press, 1989), pp. 127–8.

3 Lasker and Borg, p. 56.

4 Lasker and Borg, p. 57.
5 Williams, p. 130.
6 G. Corea, *The Mother Machine: Reproductive Technologies from Artificial Insemination to Artificial Wombs* (London: The Women's Press, 1985), p. 175.
7 Lasker and Borg, p. 56.
8 A. Fisher, *IVF: The Critical Issues* (Melbourne: Collins Dove, 1989), p. 25.
9 Williams, p. 131.
10 Lasker and Borg, p. 57.
11 Voluntary Licensing Authority (1988), Guideline 12.
12 C. Crowe, 'Women want it', p. 91.
13 Crowe, p. 91.
14 Glazer and Cooper, *Without Child*, pp. 172-4.
15 Williams, p. 136.

Chapter 4 Risks and successes

1 Fisher, *IVF: The Critical Issues*, pp. 77-8.
2 Fisher, p. 77.
3 G. B. Ellis, 'Infertility and the role of the Federal Government' in D. M. Bartels et al., *Beyond Baby M: Issues in New Reproductive Techniques* (Clifton, NJ: Humana Press, 1990), p. 117.
4 H. W. Jones and P. A. W. Rogers in C. Wood and A. Trounson (eds), *Clinical In Vitro Fertilisation* (2nd edn; London: Springer-Verlag, 1989), p. 53.
5 D. H. Barlow et al. in P. L. Matson and B. A. Lieberman (eds), *Clinical IVF Forum: Current Views in Assisted Reproduction* (Manchester: Manchester University Press, 1990), p. 63.
6 Françoise Laborie, 'Looking for mothers, you only find fetuses' in Patricia Spallone and Deborah Lynn Steinberg (eds), *Made to Order: The Myth of Reproductive and Genetic Progress* (Oxford: Pergamon Press, 1987), p. 49.
7 Wood and Trounson, p. 57.
8 Voluntary Licensing Authority, *Report* (1991), p. 14.
9 Human Fertilisation and Embryology Authority, *Annual Report* (1992), p. 10, Table 3.

Chapter 5 Feminist critiques of the NRTs and of IVF

1 M. Berer in *Spare Rib*, 151 (February 1985), p. 12.
2 S. G. Post and B. Andolsen, 'Recent works on reproductive technology', *Religious Studies Review*, 15 (1989), pp. 201–8.
3 J. Wacjman, *Feminism Confronts Technology* (Oxford: Polity Press, 1991), pp. 58–60.
4 J. Finkelstein, 'Women, pregnancy and childbirth' in J. A. Scutt (ed.), *The Baby Machine: Reproductive Technology and the Commercialisation of Motherhood* (London: Green Print, 1990), p. 3.
5 J. Raymond, 'Preface' in G. Corea et al., *Man-Made Women: How New Reproductive Technologies Affect Women* (London: Hutchinson, 1985), p. 12.
6 M. Daly, *Gyn/Ecology: The Metaethics of Radical Feminism* (Boston: Beacon Press, 1978), second passage, *passim*.
7 Corea, *The Mother Machine*, pp. 112–13.
8 F. V. Price, 'The management of uncertainty in obstetric practice: ultrasonography, in vitro fertilisation and embryo transfer' in McNeil, Varcoe and Yearley (eds), *The New Reproductive Technologies*, p. 152.
9 R. P. Petchesky, *Abortion and Women's Choice: The State, Sexuality and Reproductive Freedom* (London: Verso, 1986), pp. vii–viii.
10 Post and Andolsen, p. 212.
11 T. McCormack, 'The bias of bioethics' in D. Macniven (ed.), *Moral Expertise: Studies in Practical and Professional Ethics* (London/New York: Routledge, 1990), p. 148.
12 M. A. Warren, 'IVF and women's interests: an analysis of women's concerns', *Bioethics*, 1 (1988), pp. 53–4.
13 R. Rowland, 'Technology and motherhood: reproductive choice reconsidered', *Signs*, 12 (1987), pp. 512–18.
14 J. Hanmer and P. Allen, 'Reproductive engineering: the final solution?' in L. Birke and S. West, *Alice Through the Microscope: The Power of Science over Women's Lives* (London: Virago, 1980), p. 225.
15 D. Steinberg, 'The depersonalisation of women through the administration of "in vitro fertilisation"' in McNeil, Varcoe and Yearley, pp. 74–122.

16 R. P. Petchesky, 'Foetal images: the power of visual culture in the politics of reproduction' in Stanworth, *Reproductive Technologies*, p. 63.

17 Warren, pp. 53–4.

Chapter 6 IVF and natural law

1 E. D'Arcy, 'Natural law' in W. Reich (ed.), *Encyclopedia of Bioethics* (New York: The Free Press, 1978), p. 1131.

2 E. P. Flynn, *Human Fertilization In Vitro: A Catholic Perspective* (Lanham, MD/New York/London: University Press of America, 1984), p. 7.

3 J. Fletcher, 'Anglican theology and the ethics of natural law' in J. C. Bennett (ed.), *Christian Social Ethics in a Changing World: An Ecumenical Theological Enquiry* (New York: Association Press, 1966), p. 316.

4 C. Ryan, 'The traditional concept of natural law: an interpretation' in I. Evans (ed.), *Light on the Natural Law* (London: Burns and Oates, 1965), pp. 13, 15–16.

5 Ryan, p. 15.

6 K. T. Kelly, 'The Embryo Research Bill: some underlying ethical issues', *The Month*, 3 (March 1990), p. 119.

7 T. O'Connell, *Principles for a Catholic Morality* (New York: Seabury Press, 1978), p. 175.

8 Kelly, p. 119.

9 Cited in Fletcher, p. 323.

10 Flynn, cited in Fletcher, p. 323.

Chapter 7 IVF and the Bible

1 S. Hauerwas, *Suffering Presence: Theological Reflections on Medicine, the Mentally Handicapped, and the Church* (Edinburgh: T. and T. Clark, 1986), p. 143.

2 Flynn, pp. 1–7.

3 P. Simmons, *Birth and Death: Bioethical Decision-Making* (Philadelphia: Westminster Press, 1983), chs 2 and 5.

Chapter 8 IVF: towards responsibility

1 A. Jonsen, *Responsibility in Modern Religious Ethics* (Lexington: Corpus Books, 1968), p. 206.
2 Jonsen, ch. 6.
3 H. Jonas, *The Imperative of Responsibility: In Search of an Ethics for the Technological Age* (Chicago/London: University of Chicago Press, 1984), pp. 4ff.

Chapter 9 Some IVF participants

1 The Warnock Report, pp. 15–16.
2 See J. Lorber, 'Choice, gift, or patriarchal bargain?: women's consent to in vitro fertilization in male infertility' in H. B. Holmes and L. M. Purdy, *Feminist Perspectives in Medical Ethics* (Bloomington/Indianapolis: Indiana University Press, 1992), pp. 169–80.
3 O. M. T. O'Donovan, *Begotten or Made?* (Oxford: Clarendon Press, 1984), p. 49.
4 Interim Licensing Authority, *The Fifth Report of the Interim Licensing Authority for Human In Vitro Fertilisation and Embryology* (London, 1990), p. 15.
5 R. Snowden, G. D. Mitchell and E. Snowden, *Social Implications of Artificial Insemination by Semen Donor* (privately circulated, 1983), pp. 1–4.
6 J. Brandon, 'Telling the AID child', *Adoption and Fostering* 1 (1979), pp. 13–14.
7 D. G. Jones, *Manufacturing Humans: The Challenge of the New Reproductive Technologies* (Leicester: Inter-Varsity Press, 1987), p. 173.
8 P. Huerre, 'Psychological aspects of semen donation' in G. David and W. S. Price (eds), *Human Artificial Insemination and Semen Preservation* (New York/London: Plenum Press, 1980), pp. 461–5.
9 C. Alexandre, 'Difficulties encountered by infertile couples facing AID' in David and Price, pp. 131–4.

Chapter 10 IVF and embryo research

1 D. Atkinson, 'Some theological perspectives on the human embryo', *Ethics in Medicine*, 2 (1986), pp. 8–10.

2 C. R. Austin, *Human Embryos: The Debate on Assisted Reproduction* (Oxford: Oxford University Press, 1989), p. 31.

3 M. Seller, 'The human embryo: a scientist's point of view', *Bioethics*, 2/3 (April 1993), pp. 136–7.

4 A. Caplan, 'Arguing with success: is in vitro fertilization research or therapy?' in D. M. Bartels et al. (eds), *Beyond Baby M: Issues in New Reproductive Techniques* (Clifton, NJ: Humana Press, 1990), p. 161.

5 Seller, p. 137.

6 Downie, *Babymaking*, p. 46.

7 Downie, p. 28.

8 Instruction, *Respect for Human Life*, I. 4.

9 The Declaration of Helsinki, in A. S. Duncan et al., *Dictionary of Medical Ethics* (2nd edn, London: Darton, Longman and Todd, 1981), pp. 132–5.

10 The Warnock Report, p. 62.

11 The Warnock Report, p. 60.

12 O'Donovan, *Begotten or Made?*, p. 59.

13 The Warnock Report, p. 60.

Chapter 11 Human fertilization and embryology: Act and Authority

1 The principal sources used in this chapter are: *The Sixth Report of the Interim Licensing Authority for Human In Vitro Fertilisation and Embryology* (London, 1991); Human Fertilisation and Embryology Authority, *Annual Report* (London, 1992); *Second Annual Report* (London, 1993); *Code of Practice* (London, n.d.); *Code of Practice* (London, 1993); D. Morgan and R. G. Lee, *Blackstone's Guide to the Human Fertilisation and Embryology Act 1990: Abortion and Embryo Research, The New Law* (London: Blackstone Press, 1991).

Chapter 12 *The wider society*

1 S. Sherwin, 'Feminist ethics and new reproductive technologies' in Overall (ed.), *The Future of Human Reproduction*, pp. 259–60.
2 W. B. Jones and A. W. Matthews, 'Towards a taxonomy of technology and religion' in F. Ferre (ed.), *Research in Philosophy and Technology: Technology and Religion*, 10 (Greenwich, CT: JAI Press, 1990), pp. 3–23.
3 M. McNeil, 'Reproductive technologies' in McNeil, Varcoe and Yearley (eds), *The New Reproductive Technologies*, p. 1.
4 J. A. Matteo, 'Technology, power and the state' in E. H. Baruch et al. (eds), *Embryos, Ethics and Women's Rights: Exploring the New Reproductive Technologies* (New York/London: Haworth Press, 1988), pp. 211–14.
5 D. J. Fasching, 'The dialectic of apocalypse and utopia in the theological ethics of Jacques Ellul' in Ferre, pp. 149–65.
6 B. K. Rothman, 'Reproductive technology and the commodification of life' in Baruch et al., pp. 95–100.
7 J. G. Raymond, 'Reproductive gifts and gift giving: the altruistic woman', *Hastings Center Report*, 20 (November/December 1990), pp. 7–11.

Index